Michael & Sue Price

# Internet for Seniors

## Third Edition

For the Over 50s

In easy steps is an imprint of In Easy Steps Limited
Southfield Road · Southam
Warwickshire CV47 0FB · United Kingdom
www.ineasysteps.com

Third Edition

Notice of Liability
Every effort has been made to ensure that this book contains accurate
and current information. However, In Easy Steps Limited and the
author shall not be liable for any loss or damage suffered by readers
as a result of any information contained herein.

Trademarks
Microsoft® and Windows® are registered trademarks of Microsoft
Corporation. All other trademarks are acknowledged as belonging to
their respective companies.

In Easy Steps Limited supports The Forest Stewardship Council (FSC),
the leading international forest certification organisation. All our titles
that are printed on Greenpeace approved FSC certified paper carry the
FSC logo.

**MIX**
Paper from
responsible sources
**FSC**
www.fsc.org  **FSC® C020837**

Printed and bound in the United Kingdom

ISBN 978-1-84078-400-8

# Contents

## 4    Chess and Bridge    49

## 5    Internet Entertainment    67

# 1 Get Started

*This chapter outlines the Internet and the World Wide Web, it discusses the facilities you need to get on the Internet from your computer, and introduces Internet Explorer and the alternative browsers that give you safe and secure access to the Internet.*

# The Internet

**Beware**

There is no overseer, or manager, for the Internet, so Internet security is provided by software installed on your computer (see page 214).

The Internet (Interconnected Network) is a global network connecting millions of computers, organized into thousands of commercial, academic, domestic and government networks located in over 100 countries. The Internet is sometimes called the Information Highway, because it provides the transportation and routing for the information exchanged between the connected computers.

The computers on the Internet are connected by a variety of methods, including the telephone system, wired networks, wireless (radio) networks, cable TV and even satellite.

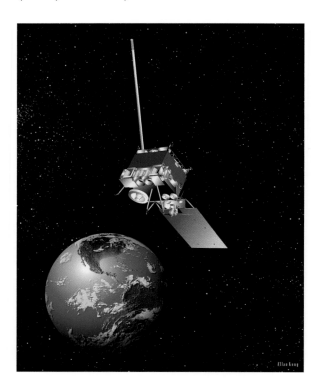

**Hot tip**

The computers on the Internet are known as hosts or servers, and they create exchanges for news, views and data of all kinds.

Some sections are commercial, others are academic or government, but no single organization owns the Internet as a whole. It is simply made up of individual, independent networks and computers, whose owners and operators decide which Internet methods to use and which local services to offer to the global Internet community.

# Internet Services

The services offered could include one or more of these:

- Electronic mail (email)

  This allows you and other Internet users to send and receive messages.

- FTP (File Transfer Protocol)

  This allows your computer to retrieve files from a remote computer and view or save them onto your computer.

- Internet Service Providers (ISPs)

  These, as the name suggests, provide points of access to the Internet. You need an ISP account, plus the means of connecting your computer to one of their computers.

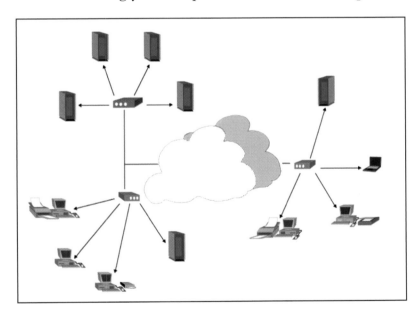

- World Wide Web (WWW)

  Also known as the Web, this is made up of collections of files and documents that may include images, animation, video and hyperlinks to other documents. These can be on the same computer, or on different computers, anywhere on the Internet.

**Don't forget**

There are other ways to connect to the Internet that don't require a computer, such as by cell phone, or a PDA device.

**Don't forget**

A location on the Web is known as a website. It will have a home page, the document that you see when you enter the site. It might have additional documents (web pages) and files, usually related to the main theme or focus.

**Hot tip**

To visit a website, and follow the hyperlinks in the web pages, you will need an Internet browser (see page 17).

**Hot tip**

If you are planning to access the Internet from someone else's computer, it should already be set up for Internet access, though you will need the sign on code and password for your email account.

**Beware**

Don't assume that your supplier will have provided the best choice in every instance. Often, there will be 90 day trial versions of software, or lite (limited function) editions and you must pay extra for the full product. You may find cheaper alternatives, and even free options, if you search on the Internet.

# Requirements

To connect to the Internet, there are a number of things that you'll require:

**1** A computer equipped for use on the Internet. In this book we assume that you are using a Windows-based PC (see page 13)

**2** A means of connecting your PC (or PCs) to the computers at your ISP, including the hardware components, the communications software and the cabling, or phone links

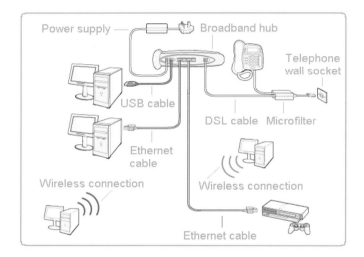

**3** An ISP account that will provide access to the Internet. You may also need email services, which would normally use the same account

**4** Appropriate software on your computer, to exchange information with other computers on the Internet, and to send and receive emails

We'll look at each of these in turn, so you will know all the tasks that are involved in setting up your computer, and can identify what remains to be done.

# Internet Enabled Computer

If you purchased your computer within the last three or four years, it will almost certainly be adequate for most activities on the Internet. If you have an older computer, review these hardware and software specifications to see if it will meet your needs for Internet access.

### Processor
If your computer has a Pentium 1GHz processor, or anything faster than this, you won't be restricted by the power of your computer.

### Operating System
While any version of Windows will allow you to access the Internet, for the best security you should upgrade to the most current version, e.g. Windows 7. The Home Premium and Ultimate editions are recommended for home users, and Professional or Enterprise for businesses.

### Memory
Although it is possible to run your computer with less memory, your use of the Internet will be smoother and more effective if you have memory of 2GB or more installed.

### Hard Disk Drive
Check the free space on your hard drive. If there is 20GB or more available, you'll have no problems with disk space. Any less, and you might wish to consider replacing the drive, or simply adding a second drive.

### Display Monitor and Adapter
To take full advantage of the Internet, you should preferably have a 17" monitor or larger, capable of displaying Hicolor (16bit), Trucolor (24bit) or better, at a resolution of 1024 x 768 pixels. CRT monitors and flat screen LCD displays are equally suitable, though the latter are much easier to house.

**Don't forget**

Other requirements include a soundcard, speakers and DVD drive, if you want to play videos on your computer. You may also want a printer, and perhaps a scanner, but these are not essential for accessing the Internet.

**Hot tip**

To check the computer specifications, open Control Panel, click System and Maintenance and then System, to see the operating system level, the processor type and the memory installed.

**Don't forget**

Open the Computer folder and select the individual drive to check the size and the space available on that drive, displayed in the Details panel at the foot of the window.

**Hot tip**

You may pay as you go, for the call or connection time, or pay a fixed fee for a specified maximum number of hours, depending on which works out most economical for your average amount of usage.

**Beware**

You may have a Wireless connection with ADSL Broadband. This still uses the normal telephone cables to connect to the ISP, but allows you to access the router from anywhere in your home. However, this is not full wireless connection.

# Connection Types

The type of connection you need depends on how much use you will be making of Internet access. There are four main options, though not all are available in every region.

### Dial-up

This is a low speed, low cost method for limited usage (less than say, five hours per week). It uses a Modem in your computer, which connects to a standard telephone socket. Your normal phone line is unavailable for incoming or outgoing calls while you are using the Internet.

### ADSL Broadband

This offers higher speed and supports a higher level of usage. It uses an ADSL modem attached to your computer or, alternatively, a separate device known as a router. It makes use of your telephone connection, but transfers data in a digital format that allows the line to remain available for normal incoming or outgoing calls. You can, if you wish, leave your computer connected all the time.

### Cable TV

If your area has Cable TV services, these may offer a broadband connection. This operates in a similar fashion to ADSL Broadband, but is independent of your telephone line.

### Satellite

If there are no ADSL or cable services available in your area, satellite services can provide you with a permanent 2-way connection to the Internet that uses no telephone line. All you need is an interface box, and a small satellite dish connected to your computer. There are services designed for home use, a local community or businesses.

### Wireless

This is the type of connection you use with a laptop computer (or a handheld unit) when you are away from home, at an airport, hotel or Internet cafe. Your computer will have a wireless modem, and the organization that you are visiting will provide the wireless access point which, in turn, connects to the Internet.

# ISP Account

Having decided on the type of connection that meets your needs, you need an Internet Service Provider to complete the connection. There are several ways to identify ISPs:

- Ask friends and family which ISP they use

- Check for pre-installed links on your computer for setting up a well-known ISP, such as AOL or MSN

- Look for CDs for ISPs, in the information supplied with your computer, to get onscreen instructions

- Check at your local bookstore, supermarket or computer store, for ISP CDs and special offers

If you have access to the Internet on another system, visit a website that can help you choose a suitable service. For example, to choose a broadband service:

1. Go to www.theispguide.com/ for details of North American providers

2. Search in your location by specifying the Area Code, or City and State

3. ISPs for the UK and Australia can also be listed with this guide

## Don't forget

Check that your selected ISP will provide a modem, router or other hardware components that are needed to set up your broadband account.

## Don't forget

There are similar ISP lists available for other regions and countries.

# Set Up Internet Connection

In most cases, the instructions you require to set up and configure your Internet connection will be made available by the Internet Service Provider you have selected. However, Windows does provide guidance for creating the connection. This may be useful when you are setting up, for example, a simple dial-up connection, perhaps using the ISP account from your previous computer. To run this wizard:

## Don't forget

There's usually a setup CD, available from your ISP, that will take you, step by step, through the connection process, with explanations at each stage. This will avoid setting up your connection manually.

**1** Select Start, type network, and select Network and Sharing Center

**2** Select to Set up a new connection or network

**3** Choose your required connection option, for example Dial-up, then click the Next button and enter the phone number, user name and account password

## Hot tip

In this example, a dial-up network connection for NetZero is being set up. This provides a dial-up service that is free apart from the telephone line charges. This could be useful as a backup, or for lower levels of usage.

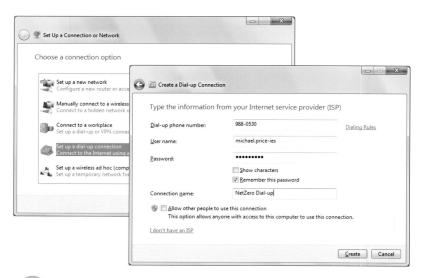

**4** Click Connect to complete the connection setup

# Start Your Browser

The first step in browsing the Internet is to start your Internet browser software. By default, this will be Internet Explorer, though you can choose an alternative (see page 19). There are two methods that you might use:

**1** Click Start, All Programs, and then select your browser from the Start menu

**2** If the browser has been pinned to the taskbar, select its icon

In either case, the browser will be opened. If it is not already active, your connection to the Internet will be established. When the connection completes, the default web page, in this case Google.com, will be displayed.

This is known as your Home page, and it appears whenever you start your browser, or press the Home button on the toolbar. The page address is specified when your software is installed or re-configured, and is usually a news page chosen by your ISP. However, you can select the web page (or web pages) that you'd prefer (see page 34).

(see page 34).

**Hot tip**

To add your browser to the taskbar, right-click its entry in the Start menu and select Pin to Taskbar.

**Hot tip**

Default means a particular value or setting (in this case a web page) that is assigned automatically, and remains in effect until you cancel or change it.

# Internet Explorer Window

Your browser is the key component in any Internet activity, so you should become familiar with all of its features.

Title bar — Address bar — Tab bar — Toolbar — Search box

Favorites button

Quick Tab button

Selected Tab

Web Page Window

Status bar — Security Settings — Scroll bars — Zoom

To add extra buttons, or to remove buttons, from the toolbar:

**1** Right-click the toolbar, select Customize, and then Add or Remove Commands

**2** Select a toolbar button and click Add or Remove, as appropriate

# Other Browser Software

The browser supplied with Windows is Internet Explorer, the version depends on which release of Windows you have. However, there are alternative browsers. The Browsers List at www.webdevelopersnotes.com/design/browsers_list.php3, for example, lists 42, of which 27 run under Windows, 19 under Linux or Unix, and 19 under Macintosh. Or you can choose from the main browsers listed at www.browserchoice.eu.

Don't forget

In Europe, Microsoft offers a Browser Ballot, via Windows Update, to give a choice of browsers that could replace the supplied Internet Explorer.

1. Select the Download link for one of the browsers for your operating system, for example Mozilla Firefox

2. Follow the prompts to install the selected browser

3. When you start the new browser, you'll be asked if you want to make it the new default for web pages

Hot tip

You are able to install a number of browsers on your system, but one of them will be specified as the default web browser.

4. Click No to keep Internet Explorer as the default

# Alternative Browsers

**1** This shows the Opera browser, with the same set of web pages shown for Internet Explorer (see page 18)

**2** This shows the Mozilla Firefox browser, again with the same set of web pages displayed

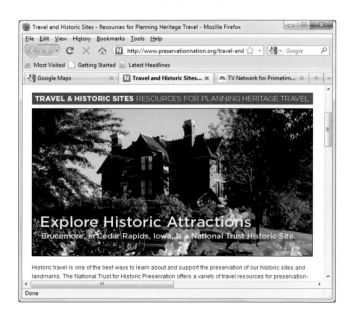

# 2 Browse the Internet

The Internet is an enormous library of information, but it is not well organized at all, so you have to locate what you need, by name, through links or by searching using descriptive keywords, taking full advantage of the capabilities of your browsing software.

# Web Page Address

To find your way around the Internet, you need to understand web page addresses. For example, the sample home page (see page 17) has this web address:

 http://www.**google.com**/index.html

This address is made up of several parts:

- http://                    Indicates web pages
- www.google.com             The web server name
- index.html                 The web page name

The web server name is, itself, made up of several parts:

- www                        Indicates a host computer
- google                     The company or owner name
- com                        The website type

You will encounter various other website types, such as:

- com                        Commercial website
- org                        Organization – usually nonprofit
- edu                        Education (e.g. university)
- gov                        Government department

There are international versions of these website types, incorporating a country identification, for example:

- com.au, org.au, edu.au, gov.au     Australia
- co.in, org.in, ac.in, gov.in       India
- co.uk, org.uk, ac.uk, gov.uk       United Kingdom

There are also various website types that are not associated with any particular country:

- biz, info, me, net                 Business related

## Don't forget

The web server name incorporates the Domain name, which consists of owner name and website type, in this case google.com. Other examples of domain names are:
microsoft.com
preservationnation.org

**22**

## Beware

Individuals, as well as companies, can register domain names of many different types, so the name itself does not tell you anything about the owner.

## Hot tip

Although there are general similarities, the naming is not entirely consistent, country to country, e.g. using co instead of com, and ac (Academic) instead of edu.

# Open a Web Page

If you find a web page address in an article or advertisement, or are given a web address by a friend, you can direct the browser to display that page. For example, to display the World of Playing Cards web page, www.wopc.co.uk:

**1** Start Internet Explorer (see page 17), if required, and click the address bar area. The address is highlighted

**2** Type the required web page address. This replaces the existing highlighted address

**3** Press Enter, or click the blue arrow button, to display the required page

**4** You may see a progress indicator on the Status bar, depending on how quickly the web page loads

# Links

When you've displayed one web page, you can usually go on to another page without having to type a web page address. Instead, you click on items on the current page that have web addresses associated with them. These items are called Links (or Hyperlinks). They are often descriptive text, underlined and colored blue, or red, as in the example.

To confirm whether a part of the page is a link:

1  Place the mouse pointer over the item. If it is a link, the pointer changes to a hand symbol, to indicate that there is a link address

2  The target location is shown on the status bar

3  Sometimes the link is associated with a graphic image, and again the pointer changes to a hand

4  The image may also have a descriptive Tool Tip associated with it

5  Select one of the counties listed for location specific articles and stories about playing cards

# Follow Links

**1** Click the Alphabetical Index of Card Games link at www.pagat.com to show the A to Z web page

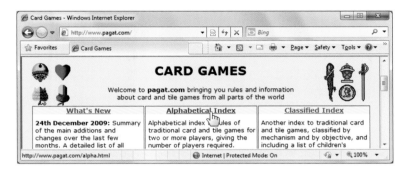

**Don't forget**

A link can point to a web page on a different site, or a web page on the same site, or a different location within the web page (as indicated by the #label appended to the web page address).

**2** Click the H link to move down the same web page to the location www.pagat.com/alpha.html#h

**Hot tip**

The slider on the scroll bar indicates where you are on the page. You can click and drag this slider to reposition your view.

**3** Click any link to visit that web page

When you visit a location the color of the link changes, typically from blue to purple, providing a visual cue for future visits, to remind you that you have previously followed that particular link.

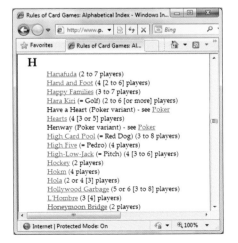

**Don't forget**

The hyperlink color will remain changed, even when you restart Internet Explorer, until you clear the browsing history, or the records expire.

# Address Help

Internet Explorer offers you help with entering web page addresses, in several ways.

1 Click the arrow at the end of the Address bar, to see a list of web page addresses that you have typed previously, and click the one that you want

2 If you start typing an address (as on page 22), Internet Explorer lists previously visited web pages that match the part entered so far. As soon as you see the required web page, click the entry to open it

3 Type the company, or organization, name on the address bar, and then press Ctrl+Enter. For example:

# Add to Favorites

When you visit a web page that you find useful, make it easy to find at another time by adding it to your list of favorites.

1. While viewing the web page, click the Favorites button and then click Add to Favorites

**Hot tip**

Pages you visit every day can become your home page, so they open whenever Internet Explorer opens. See page 17.

2. The title of the page is suggested as the name, or you can type another, perhaps more descriptive, name

**Don't forget**

Press the New Folders button to create a subfolder in the Favorites list. Click the down-arrow to select a subfolder in which to store the web page details.

3. Click Add to put the page details onto the main list

4. Click the Favorites button and select the Favorites tab to display the list

5. Select any page you wish to visit (click the blue arrow to open a new tab for the page)

**Hot tip**

If you forgot to add a web page, and you want to find it again, click the History tab and you'll see the pages you have visited over a recent period of time.

# Searching

If you have no idea of the correct website, Internet Explorer will carry out a search on your behalf.

**1** Click in the Search box to the right of the address bar, type some keywords appropriate to the website you want, and press Enter

**2** Internet Explorer uses your default search engine to find web pages that are related to your search terms

**3** Scroll down or page forward, as required, until you find the website you want, then click the header

**4** Press the Back button to return to the search results

Hot tip

As you type, the search engine may offer suggestions of search terms for you to select and amend.

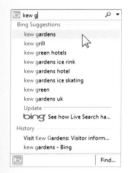

Hot tip

Press Ctrl+E to position the typing cursor in the Search box, without having to use the mouse.

Don't forget

Internet Explorer sets the default as Live Search, but you can add additional search providers, or change the default provider.

# Add Search Providers

If you prefer to use different search providers, you can make additional providers available, and change the default.

**1** Click the down arrow next to the search box, and select Find More Providers, to open the Add-ons Gallery for Search Providers

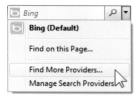

**Hot tip**

Select other countries and languages to display the associated search providers. The default is the location you specify in the Control Panel e.g. United States (English).

**2** Locate the search provider you require, and click the button to Add to Internet Explorer

**3** Click the box to Make this my default search provider, if desired, and then click the Add button

**4** Select and add other search providers you may want to use

**5** In future sessions, display the list and select an entry to make it your choice for that session

**Don't forget**

Select Manage Search providers, to disable search suggestions, change the listing order, remove an entry or set a new default.

# Specific Searches

**1** By default, searches will be for relevant web pages

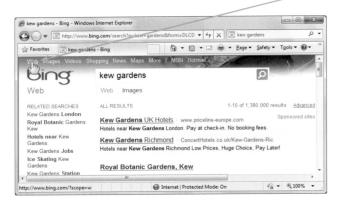

**2** Click Images to search for relevant images, which will be displayed as thumbnails

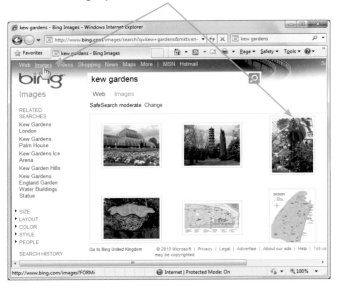

**3** Click a thumbnail and select Full-size to view the image, or right-click and choose Save picture as, to capture a copy

# Open New Tab

Tabs allow you to have more than one web page open at the same time, without having to open a separate copy of your browser. To open a new tab:

**1** Click New Tab on the tab row (or press Ctrl+T)

**2** A New Tab opens, with suggested actions, and the Quick Tabs button is displayed on the tab bar

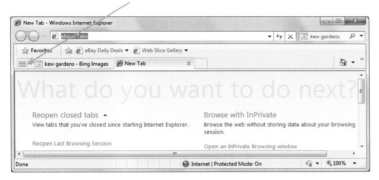

**3** Reopen tabs that you have previously closed, in the current session or in an earlier session

**4** Open a web service with text copied from a web page

**5** Type, or paste, a web page address onto the address bar

## Hot tip

You can turn on InPrivate Browsing, which lets you surf the Internet without leaving traces, by automatically clearing your web history when you close the session.

**31**

## Don't forget

The title for each page appears on the appropriate tab, while the title for the currently selected tab appears on the Internet Explorer titlebar.

# Using Tabs

**1** Type the web page location on the address bar, with the current tab displayed, then press Alt+Enter

**2** Right-click a hyperlink on the web page and select to Open in New tab

**3** Hold down the Ctrl key as you left-click a hyperlink on the web page

**4** Click the Quick Tabs button to review all the tabbed pages, and select one you want

# Close Tabs

Having opened a number of tabs, you can close them individually or as groups.

**1** Click the [X] on the currently selected tab (or press Ctrl+W) to close that tab

**2** Right-click any tab and select Close Tab

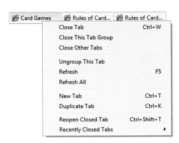

**3** Select Close This Tab Group to close all associated tabs, or Close Other Tabs (and leave the selected tab open)

**4** If you change your mind, select Reopen Closed Tab to open the last one closed, or select Recently Closed Tabs to select one from the list

**5** You can refresh the selected tab (or all tabs), ungroup the tab, or duplicate the tab

**6** Click the Close button (or press Alt+F4) to close Internet Explorer

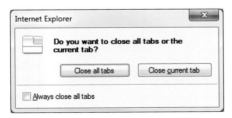

**7** Select Close all tabs, and end the browsing session

**8** You can Reopen Last Browsing Session when you select New Tab (see page 31) the next time you open Internet Explorer

You can select the [X] button on any Quick Tabs thumbnail to close it, or right-click a thumbnail to display the menu of open and close options.

## Hot tip

To save all open tabs, and make them available for reload as a group, click Favorites, click the arrow next to Add to Favorites (see page 27) and select Add Current Tabs to Favorites.

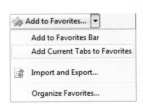

# Change Home Page

You can change the web page used as the initial page when Internet Explorer starts up.

**Hot tip**

If you find a web page that would make a good home page, you can specify it to add to, or replace, the one that is currently defined.

**1** Open your preferred web page, PBS TV for example, by typing its URL on the address bar (see page 23)

**2** At www.pbs.org, click the arrow next to the Home Page button

**3** Select the option to Add or Change Home Page

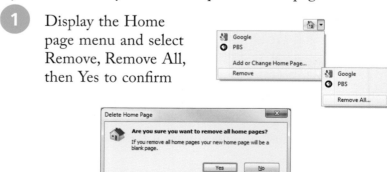

**Don't forget**

Select Use this web page as your only home page, to replace the existing home page with the currently displayed web page.

**4** Choose an option, for example Use this web page as your only home, and click Yes to apply the change

The specified web page opens automatically, when you click the Home button, or whenever you start Internet Explorer.

### Blank Home Page

If you decide that you do not require a home page at all:

**1** Display the Home page menu and select Remove, Remove All, then Yes to confirm

**Hot tip**

If there are multiple home page tabs, you can selectively remove some of them.

From now on, a blank web page is displayed when you start Internet Explorer, or press the Home button.

# 3 Puzzles and Solutions

*Use online reference materials to look up words, get solutions to crossword clues, locate facts or resolve anagrams. You can also use the Internet as a source of entertaining puzzles and quizzes, or to locate online books, especially the classics, which you can read and research.*

# Solve Crosswords

You might make a start by using the Internet to help you with a crossword. Suppose you have a partially solved crossword, and want to use the Internet to help complete it:

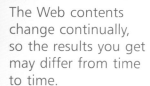
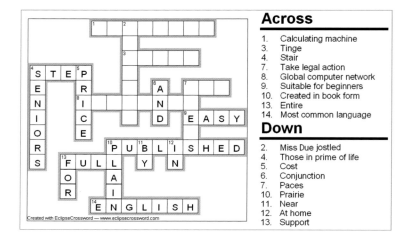

**Across**

1. Calculating machine
3. Tinge
4. Stair
7. Take legal action
8. Global computer network
9. Suitable for beginners
10. Created in book form
13. Entire
14. Most common language

**Down**

2. Miss Due jostled
4. Those in prime of life
5. Cost
6. Conjunction
7. Paces
10. Prairie
11. Near
12. At home
13. Support

**1** Type the keywords solve crossword in the Search box, and click the Search button

**2** The website at www.oneacross.com offers free help with crosswords (and anagrams and cryptograms)

# Resolve Clues

The OneAcross website allows you to enter complete clues, along with the number of letters required. For example:

**1** Type the clue Take legal action and the pattern ??? (meaning three letters, all unknown), and click Go!

Hot tip

Solve clue 7 across:
Take legal action (3)

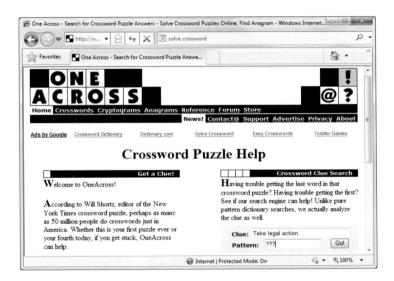

**2** The website displays the answers that it finds, with the most likely answer shown first

Don't forget

When you think you know one or more letters, replace the ?s in the appropriate positions with the expected letter. Use upper case if you are sure you have the correct letter, lower case otherwise.

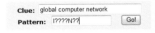

# Find Anagrams

 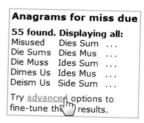
Many crosswords incorporate anagrams in the clues. The server at www.wordsmith.org/anagram helps with these.

**1** Type the anagram word or phrase (spaces will be ignored), e.g. miss due, and click Get Anagrams

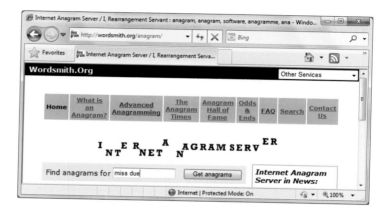

**2** The website displays all the answers that it can find. These can include multiple words, abbreviations, acronyms etc

**3** For more specific answers, use the Advanced options

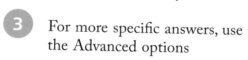

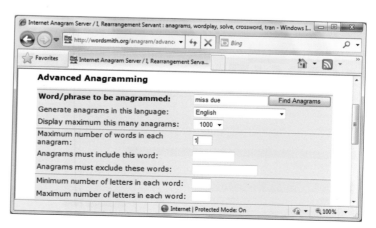

# Look Up Words

You can look up words in an online dictionary, for example:

1. Visit www.onelook.com, and type the pattern for the word, using ???s and inserting letters you know

**Hot tip**

Solve clue 1 across: Calculating machine (8)

2. OneLook defaults to All Matches, and lists the potential answers in alphabetic order

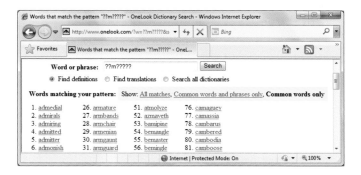

**Hot tip**

If there are many possibilities, only the first 100 are listed. Select Common Words Only, to reduce the number.

3. Add words from the clue (separated by a colon from the word pattern). The most likely will be listed first

**Beware**

Words from the clue may not help if you are completing a cryptic crossword, since they may not appear in the literal definitions.

# Crosswords Online

The Internet doesn't just help you solve crosswords, it is also a rich source of crosswords. You will soon find your own favorite sites, but to help get you started, try one of the newspapers. For example:

 Type www.washingtonpost.com/crosswords on the address bar and press Enter to open the web page

Click the Crossword button then scroll down and select the Archives & Printables link

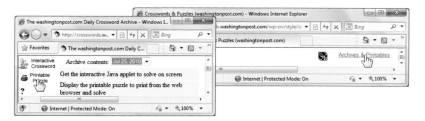

Choose a date and click the Printable Puzzle option

# Interactive Crosswords

You can complete the crosswords interactively.

**1** Select the crossword you want to complete and click Interactive Crossword

**2** If Java isn't already installed, you get a warning message

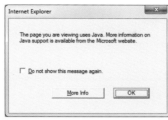

**3** Select More Info and follow the prompts to go to www.java.com and download the required version

**4** You can now enter the solutions on the screen

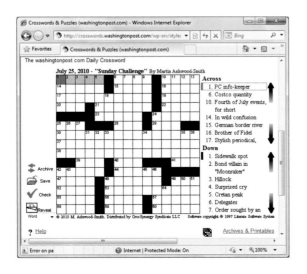

Hot tip

You may also be prompted to install the free Flash Player from Adobe Macromedia.

Don't forget

You can Save your solution periodically, and Check an answer (the incorrect letters are marked). If all else fails, click Reveal to get the selected letter or word, or answers for the whole puzzle.

# Sudoku

If you want a change from crosswords, you might switch to Sudoku. The Internet will provide advice and suggestions for completing the puzzles you find in magazines, and offer puzzles for you to play online or to print out to complete later.

**1** Go to www.websudoku.com which claims to have billions of Sudoku puzzles for you to play

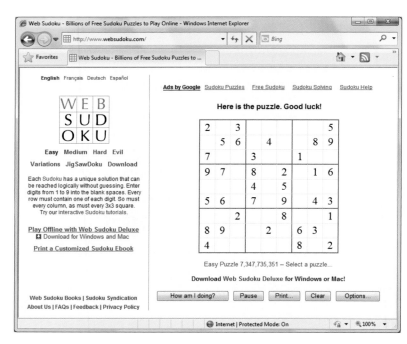

**2** Click an empty cell and type a suitable digit, based on the contents of other cells. Your entries are shown in blue italics

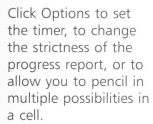
**3** To check your progress, click How am I doing? You'll be warned if you've entered a wrong number

# Solving Puzzles

Here are some useful websites that explain some of the techniques involved in solving Sudoku puzzles.

**1** At www.simetric.co.uk/sudoku you'll find three tutorials that demonstrate solving Sudoku puzzles

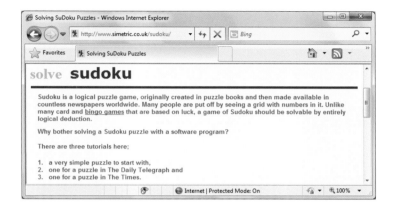

**43**

**2** There's a comprehensive guide to solving Sudoku, at www.sudoku.org.uk/PDF/Solving_Sudoku.pdf

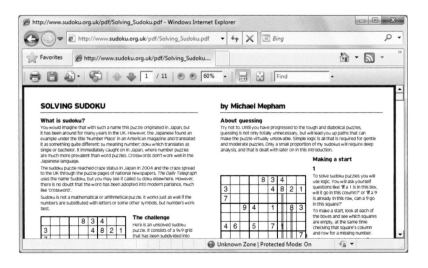

**3** Finally, for the count of valid Sudoku grids, see www.afjarvis.staff.shef.ac.uk/sudoku/sudoku.pdf

# Brain Aerobics

Many brain teaser websites are aimed at children, but you can find sites that are targeted more specifically at the 50+ age range.

Brain teasers, quizzes and games are not just for fun, or to pass the time, they also provide essential mental exercise.

**1** Search for brain teasers for seniors to find sites, such as www.clevelandseniors.com/forever/mindex.htm

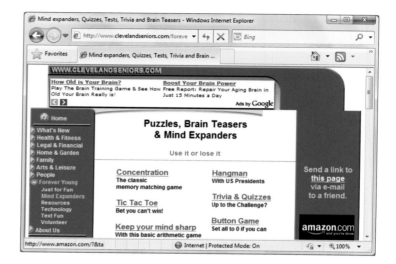

**2** Select one of the 25 or so links of Mind Expanders, for example Concentration or Trivia & Quizzes

**3** If you want more cerebral exercise, visit the website www.mensa.org and click Mensa Workout

You are given 30 minutes to answer 30 questions. Correct answers and explanations will be provided after you submit your answers.

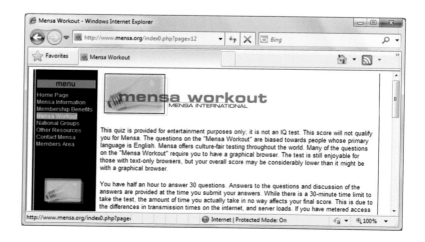

# Web Encyclopedia

To help you answer all the quizzes you find, you'll need good reference material. Make a start with the Web encyclopedia that you can edit and update, as well as reference.

**1** Go to www.wikipedia.org and choose your preferred language, e.g. English

**2** Click Log in / create account to specify your user name, password and (optionally) email address

**3** Explore the articles. Search for topics, or just click the Random Article link to see what appears

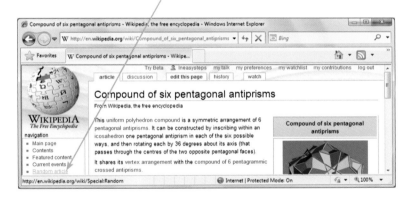

**4** Select Main page, and scroll down to list the user-maintained sister projects

# Internet Public Library

The Internet Public Library (IPL), managed and maintained by the University of Michigan School of Information, offers library services to Internet users, helping them to find, evaluate, and organize information resources.

**1** Visit www.ipl.org to see subject collections, ready reference and reading room material, etc.

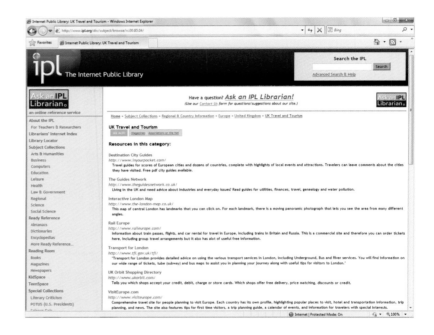

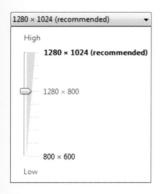

**2** There's so much information that a high screen resolution may be useful. This example is in 1280 x 1024, but this makes the text rather small

**3** Click the Zoom button at the foot of the window, to switch between 100%, 125%, and 150%, and so enlarge the view

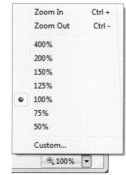

**4** Click the down-arrow to choose a preset level, between 50% and 400%, or choose a Custom value

# Online Classics

You can find the full text for many thousands of books on the Internet, in an electronic (ebook) format that is ideal for searching for particular details. They are books whose copyright has expired, and, in the main, they are classics. There are online books on Wikipedia, and on IPL, but perhaps the best source for free ebooks is Project Gutenberg.

**1**    Type www.gutenberg.org and press Enter to display the home page for the website

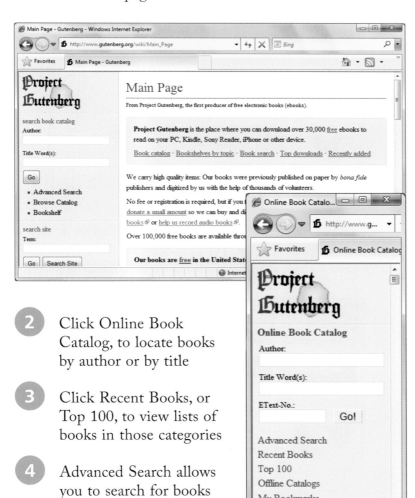

**2**    Click Online Book Catalog, to locate books by author or by title

**3**    Click Recent Books, or Top 100, to view lists of books in those categories

**4**    Advanced Search allows you to search for books with specific words or phrases in the text

47

### Hot tip

You can participate in Project Gutenberg, for example, by volunteering to proof read individual pages of books.

### Beware

If you don't live in the US, you should check the copyright laws in your country before downloading an ebook.

### Don't forget

You can also browse the database, arranged alphabetically by title or by author.

# Online Reference

There are many well known books available for reference at the Bartleby website, e.g.

Barlett's Quotations

Brewer's Phrase & Fable

Bullfinch's Mythology

Fowler's King's English

Gray's Anatomy

Harvard Classics

King James Bible

Oxford Shakespeare

Post's Etiquette

Robert's Rules of Order

Roget's Thesaurus

Strunk's Style

World Factbook

When it's reference books you want, visit the Bartleby website, where you can access a wide range of well known books.

**1** Go to www.bartleby.com and click the down-arrow next to the Search box to choose the specific type

**2** Choose a book, by Subject, Title or Author, search a section (Reference, Verse, Fiction, or Non-fiction) or select Thesaurus, Quotations or English usage

**3** When you select a specific book, the full text is provided for you to search, or read, online

# 4 Chess and Bridge

*Even if you are home alone, you can participate in games of chess or bridge over the Internet. You can play against the computer, or against human opponents. You can watch others play, historical games or live events. You'll also get lots of help on the Internet to improve your game.*

# Chess Games

If Chess is your game, you can learn tricks and techniques by studying the games between the great masters, by searching at chessgames.com.

Chessgames.com is an online database of historic chess games that help chess players to develop their game.

**1** To find a game, go to www.chessgames.com to display the home page, with several search options

You can register free, but the site does offer premium memberships at a charge of $25 per annum, allowing you to use additional game analysis tools.

**50**

**2** Type a plain text game description in the search box, for example the player names, the year, and the opening move or the result, e.g. kasparov topalov 1-0

**3** Alternatively, fill in the fields on the Advanced Search form:
- Year
- Player
- White or Black
- Opposing player
- No. of moves
- Opening (name)
- ECO code
- Result

You don't have to specify all the fields. In fact, most searches use just one or two fields to find games.

**4** Click the Find Chess Games button. The matching games will be listed. Click the game you want to see

# View Game

A chess board will be displayed, along with the list of moves that make up that particular game.

**1** Click any move to see the board configuration at that point in the game

**2** Click the arrows to step forward or backward a move at a time, or to move to the start or end point

**3** Click the Guess the Move box to run the chess training, and take the part of a player

## Beware

You'll need the Java software enabled (see page 41), and you may have to switch Java Viewers to find the one that works best on your system.

## Hot tip

The games are stored using PGN (Portable Game Notation), a simple text format which you can download and import to Chess software running on your PC.

# Play the Computer

Studying chess games is educational, but you really need to play games in order to improve your skill level. There are many websites where you can play other people, friends or strangers, but perhaps you could start off by playing against a computer program, such as Little Chess Partner.

This is a German site, with English translations, and the usual rules of chess apply, so language isn't a problem.

 Go to www.chessica.de/gamezone.html and click the first Play button, to play against the computer

### Don't forget

You'll need Java (see page 41) to play this computer. Once the pieces are displayed you can play games offline, without an active Internet connection.

**52**

### Hot tip

By default, thinking time is 10 seconds and depth of analysis is level 5. Experiment with other values, to make it easier or harder to play.

2 Click the board to start, then drag to move a (white) chess piece turn by turn. The computer won't let you make an illegal move

3 Click the Settings button to change the thinking time, or the depth of analysis, used by the computer

If you find the Little Chess Partner too challenging, there's an easier program that you can play against, to get practice.

**1** Scroll down and click the link Try This!, which appears below the chess board display

**2** Choose Black or White for the computer, and then take your turn – select a piece (which changes to purple) then click the destination to make your move. Only legal moves are allowed

**3** The Game Log records all the moves made

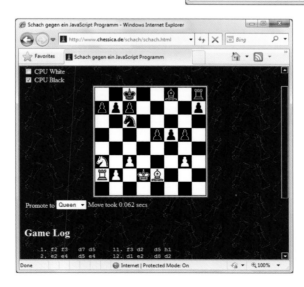

**53**

# Chess Server

**Hot tip**

On FICS, you can find casual games, or play serious chess, with other (human) players, or with a strong computer. FICS caters for all levels of player – from the very beginner, to the grand master.

To introduce yourself to the world of chess on the Internet:

**1** Visit the Free Internet Chess Server (FICS) at www. freechess.org, to register for playing online

**2** Click the Downloads link to look for a graphical interface, the easiest way to connect to FICS

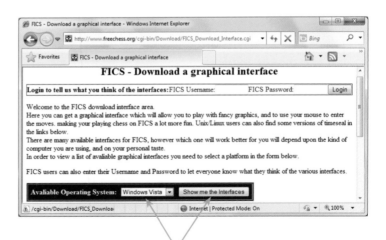

**3** Select operating system (if Windows 7 isn't offered, choose Vista) then click Show me the Interfaces

**4** Click an interface, for example: WinBoard by Tim Mann at http://www.tim-mann.org/xboard.html

# Graphical Interface

**1** Select XBoard and WinBoard, and follow the prompts to locate the download link for WinBoard

**Hot tip**

XBoard runs on Unix systems, while WinBoard runs on Windows. Tim Mann is the primary author of both applications.

**2** Download and run the WinBoard Installer program

**Don't forget**

WinBoard will be set as the viewer for .PGN files (Portable Game Notation – see page 51) and for .FEN files (Forsyth-Edwards Notation), another file type used for defining games.

**3** The WinBoard folder in Start menu, All Programs has an entry for Freechess Server – freechess.org, the FICS server, plus various other chess servers, functions, and games

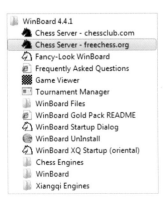

# Visit Server

You can visit the club as a guest, to help you decide if you'd like to become a full member.

**1** Select Start, All Programs, WinBoard, and click the Chess Server – freechess.org entry

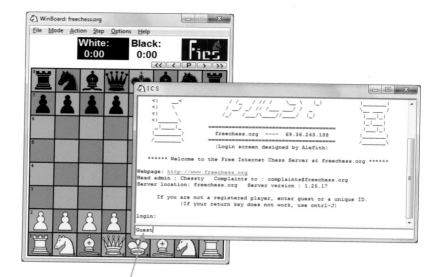

**2** Type guest and press Enter. FICS will give you a unique ID, in this case GuestMVJT

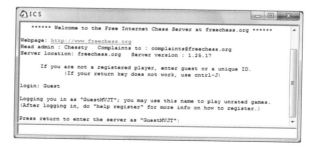

**3** Soon you'll start receiving copies of messages sent by other guests, or registered members, seeking opponents to play. Type play nn (where nn is the game number specified) to respond

# Observe Games

You may send a message to see if games are being relayed.

**1** Type tell relay listgames and press Enter

**Hot tip**

If you are told that there are no games in progress, try again later, or watch out for announcements from Relay.

**2** Type tell relay observe D11 to view that game

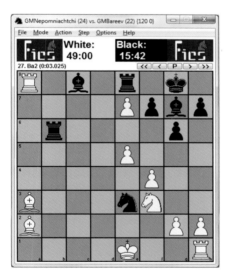

**3** The WinBoard displays the current position for the selected game, then continues to display all the moves as the game proceeds

**Don't forget**

Other useful files include:
intro_general
intro_information
intro_moving
intro_playing
register

**4** Type help intro_basics for a list of basic commands, type help intro_welcome for details, or type Exit

# Bridge Online

If bridge is your game, it is well supported on the Internet, with many websites offering help and information. You might start with the World Bridge Federation website.

**1** Visit www.worldbridge.org and click the Links entry

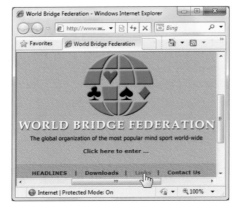

**2** Select Official Organizations and choose the zone for your region to locate the national organization

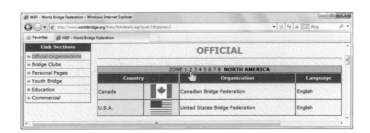

**3** Select Education from the Link Sections for useful resources identified by country and language

The national organizations also offer useful facilities. The EBU (English Bridge Union) for example runs the Really Easy Bridge programme, featuring news and events that are designed to help beginners develop their bridge.

**4** Visit www.reallyeasybridge.com to explore the options at the Really Easy Bridge website

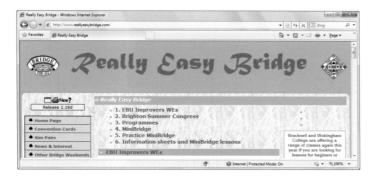

**5** Select the Point Count Table for a comprehensive analysis of opening, responses and rebids

**6** Select the Revision Pages link for details on topics, such as Stayman

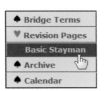

**7** Click the archive link to see previously published information

**Hot tip**

There's also lots of information on minibridge, which may be one way to introduce bridge to the grandchildren.

**Hot tip**

Select Bridge Terms for a list of definitions aimed at beginners, and ranging from Attitude signal to Reverse rebid.

# Great Bridge Links

For a more international view of bridge, you'll find an organized list of bridge-related websites at the nicely named Great Bridge Links.

**1** Visit the website www.greatbridgelinks.com

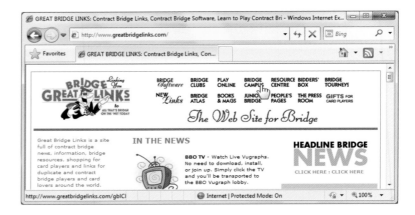

**2** Click Bridge Campus for links to websites that will help you learn (or teach) the game of bridge

**3** Click the link for a lesson for complete beginners, at Richard Pavlicek's site: www.rpbridge.net/1a00.htm

Richard Pavlicek provides a complete teaching website, at www.rpbridge.net/, with basic and advanced bridge lessons.

There are other comprehensive websites listed, for example:

1  Visit Karen's Bridge Library at home.comcast.net/~kwbridge/

# Online Bridge Clubs

When you are ready to play Bridge online, you'll find numerous websites to help you get started and to find partners.

**1** On the Great Bridge Links website, click the Play Online link for a list of online Bridge clubs

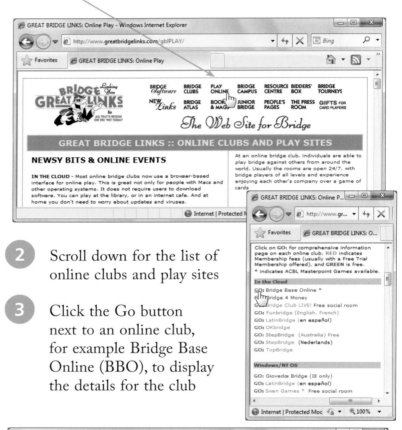

**2** Scroll down for the list of online clubs and play sites

**3** Click the Go button next to an online club, for example Bridge Base Online (BBO), to display the details for the club

4️⃣ Click the website address provided, to visit the club

**Don't forget**

You don't have to play bridge immediately. You can view current or recorded bridge games, using Vugraph broadcasts.

5️⃣ Select Vugraph Schedule to see the dates and times for tournament matches that will be broadcast

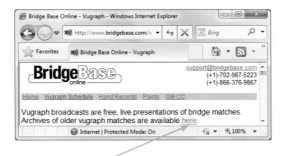

**Hot tip**

You can install the older, downloadable Bridge Base Online Windows program and use it to view downloaded Vugraph files (file type .lin).

6️⃣ Click the link to view the archives of older matches

7️⃣ Selecting View for any match will display the scoreboard (see overleaf for an example)

# View Bridge Games

**1** Open Bridge Base Online, and select a match from the vugraph archives to display the scoreboard

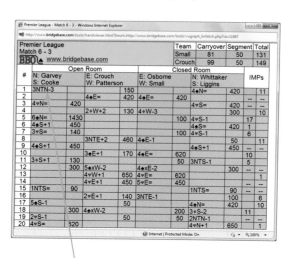

**2** Click an entry to display the hands for that game

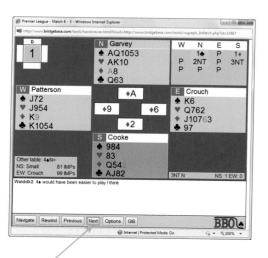

**3** Click Next to view each stage in the bidding, and to show the cards as they are played

**4** Select Navigate to display the scoreboard, the next board or the other table

| Scoreboard |
|---|
| Next board |
| Other table |
| **Navigate** |

# Log in to BBO

**1** Open Bridge Base Online and select Play Bridge Now (see page 63)

**2** If registered, enter your user name and password and click Log in

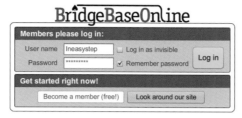

**3** If not registered, click Become a member (free!)

**4** Provide a user name and password, and add the details you wish to record, then click OK

**5** When you've logged in, select Help me find a game

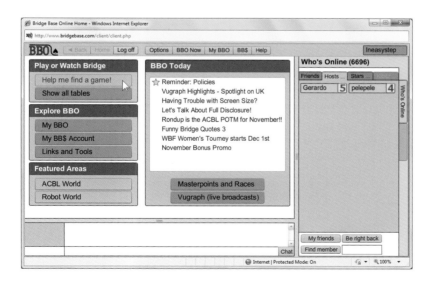

You will be able to watch games as an observer (see page 66), or join a table to play games yourself.

Hot tip

You'll be told if your user name is already in use, so you can offer a new one.

That username is not available.

Beware

The details you provide will be visible to all members, so provide limited information, until you are sure you want to remain as a member of BBO.

# Kibitz a Table

If you don't feel ready to jump right in and join a table as a player, start by watching existing games.

**1** Select Help me find a game (see page 65)

**2** The first few times, choose the entry Kibitz - take me to an interesting table

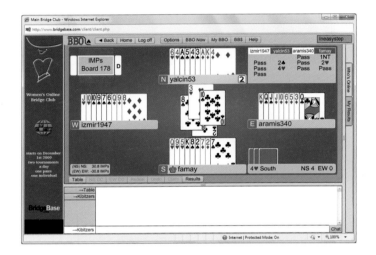

**3** When you want to leave the table, press Back

**4** Kibitz other games, or select one of the Play options, for example Take me to a table with three robots

Players, or kibitzers, may chat using the message area at the foot of the window.

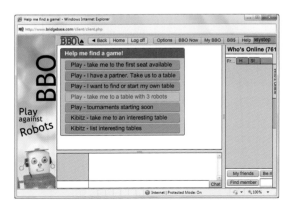

# 5 Internet Entertainment

*Use the Internet as your TV and Radio guide for regular channels or web broadcasts. Check what movies are being released, and what shows are on stage around the world. Or just relax to the sound of classical music.*

# What's on TV?

Every country has its national and regional television stations, along with numerous local stations. The Internet can help you keep track of them, and even look in on them, since many offer websites, and broadcast over the Internet.

**1** Start with a visit to a TV Station directory, such as wwitv.com, which lists live and on-demand TV broadcasts from around the world

**2** Scroll down and select a location, a region of the USA for example, to list all the TV stations available

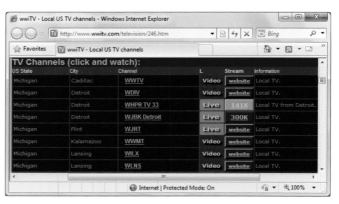

This displays a list of the prerecorded, video and live TV broadcasts available in the selected region.

**3** Choose a live TV channel, for example WVVH, and click the button to view the channel content in your browser

**4** Some live channels are restricted, e.g. BBC World News is excluded from the USA, UK and Japan

**5** Streamed TV channels may use Windows Media Player (green links) or Realplayer (blue links)

Hot tip

TV stations may provide prerecorded video programmes that can be accessed from the website, for example BBC News (recorded).

69

Don't forget

The site will detect which player is needed and, if necessary, will prompt you to install or activate it.

# Regular TV

Even if you want to watch regular TV (satellite, cable or antenna), the Internet proves useful for searching schedules.

**1** TV Zap has links to worldwide television schedules and guides, at the www.tvzap.com website

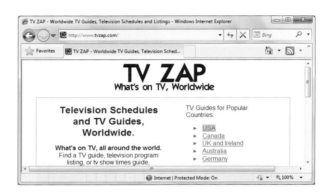

**2** Select your region or country, for example USA

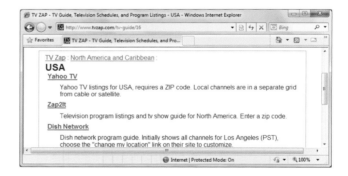

**3** Select one of the TV listings, e.g. Excite, then enter your zip code or your search criteria

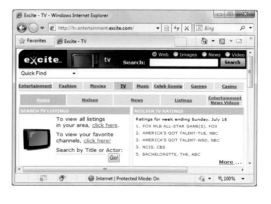

# What's on Radio?

You can find out what's on terrestrial radio stations, and listen to radio stations that broadcast over the Internet.

**1** Type the web address radiostationworld.com in the browser address bar

## Hot tip

The original address for this website was TVRadioWorld.com, and this URL will still display the website. However, the emphasis has now switched to radio broadcasts.

**2** Click the Navigate link and search for radio stations, click the down-arrow to choose the location from the list for the selected region, and then click Go

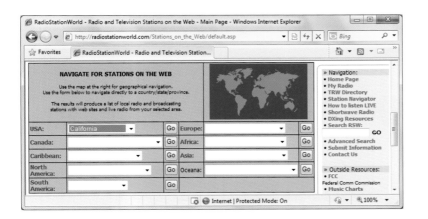

## Don't forget

As with TV over the Internet (see pages 68-9), you'll need a player to listen to the broadcast programs.

71

# Internet Radio

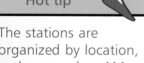
**1** Review the region of interest, to see which locations have radio stations that may be of interest

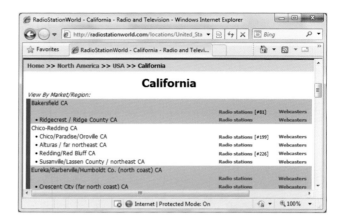

**2** Choose a particular town or district from the list, for example San Jose/Santa Cruz (South Bay area)

**3** Choose a radio station of interest in the selected area, for example KFFG in Los Altos

**4** Each station has its transmission power, location, language and type of content identified

**5** Click the speaker symbol for the radio station, to select it and listen live

### Hot tip

Click the [+] button to add the station to your MyRadio list, a sort of favorites list maintained for you by RadioStationWorld.

**6** You will be transferred to a window that identifies the media player required to play the radio stream

**7** Click the link to receive the webcast. The required media player will be installed, or initialized, and the radio station should begin playing

### Don't forget

Normally, the stations will support one or more of the same media players used for TV broadcasts (see page 69).

**8** Visit the radio station website for details of current or recently played tracks, or to download any special software required

# Visit CBS TV

## Hot tip

You can visit websites of terrestrial stations to see what features are provided.

**1** Visit the CBS TV Network website at www.cbs.com

**2** Select Full Schedule for news of what's coming up

## Don't forget

Select HD Videos and you can choose to view episodes in high quality (480), high definition (720) or full HD (1080) modes.

**3** Select Video and choose the show you want to see

**The Good Wife**
Blinded By the Lights
Ep. 1 (2:35)
Watch in: HQ HD 1080p

**4** Click an episode to view

# NBC Services

You'll find similar facilities at the NBC website.

**1** Go to the website www.nbc.com and click Schedule

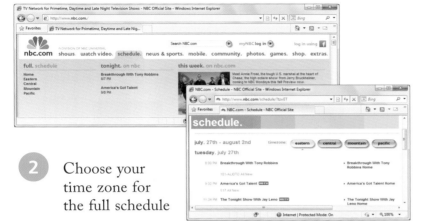

### Don't forget

You need to connect from a computer within the region, to be able to view the shows and take full advantage of the features offered.

The video you have requested is not available for your geographic region.

**2** Choose your time zone for the full schedule

**3** Click Watch Video to display a list of shows

### Hot tip

Click Shows and select a particular show for news, reviews, bios, episode guides, photos and related products.

**4** Choose a show, e.g. Days of our Lives, to list all the clips and episodes available

# Download NBC Videos

You can download NBC videos to view them later.

**1** To set up NBC Direct, go to www.nbc.com/direct

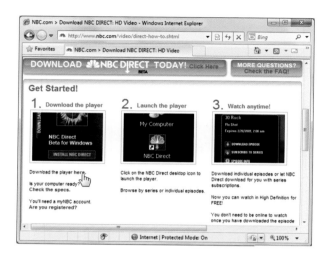

**2** Select to download the player, and follow the prompts

**3** Your system specs are checked and NBC Direct set up

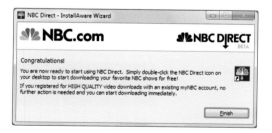

**4** Double-click the NBC Direct icon to open the NBC Video library and start downloading episodes for viewing offline

# The Movies

Maybe movies are your preference. As you'd expect, the Internet has lots to say about them. For many people, the home of movies is in Hollywood, California.

**1** You'll find a comprehensive list of Hollywood movies at the www.hollywood.com website

**2** Select the Movies tab, scroll down and click the Movie Calendar link to see what movies are scheduled

**3** Select the year and month that you want to review

**4** Select a movie title to see the synopsis and cast details

## Hot tip

For UK films, visit the movie website at britishcinemagreats.com

## Don't forget

As usual, you can right-click the link and select Open Link in New Tab, rather than a separate window.

## Hot tip

If your interest is in Indian and Asian movies, visit the alternative movie website at www. bollywoodworld.com.

# New York Theatre

If all the world's a stage for you, visit the theatre websites to see what shows are on.

**1** For New York City theatre information, including show listings, look at www.nytheatre.com

**2** Click the Venue Listings link to list all theatres, with their addresses and current/future shows

**3** Click the underlined theatre name to find out more about that venue, including details, such as exact location, travel directions and the seating plan. Click the show title to find out more about the show itself

**4**   Use Google to find a New York theatre district map

**Hot tip**

You can also switch to Google Maps and search for New York Theatres to get a map with theatre locations marked.

**5**   Select the web page from Must See New York

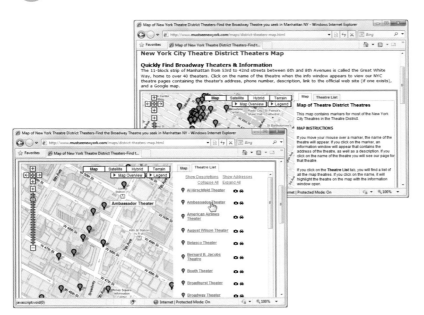

**Don't forget**

As with all Google maps, you can zoom in and out; reposition by dragging and change the map type from Street view to Satellite view.

**6**   Click Theatre List to see all the theatres on the map, and move the mouse pointer over a name to locate it

**7**   Click the theatre name or the associated marker to display an information window with phone number, address and directions

# London Theatre Guide

If you are planning to be in London, you can check what's on in the West End at the Official London Theatre site.

**1** The www.officiallondontheatre.co.uk website has theatre news, show lists, ticket purchase, awards etc

Select the Theatreland Map (pdf format) to download a copy of the map and view it in your browser with Adobe Reader.

**2** Click Select London Shows A-Z, and click the Theatreland Map entry

**3** Select the link to view the Society of London Theatre Google maps

Select a theatre name to see the address and box office number, or to request travel directions to or from the theatre.

# Classical Music Archives

If you'd simply like to relax to the sound of classical music, the Internet will not disappoint you.

**1** Visit www.classicalarchives.com to find a collection of music that you can listen to – without charge

81

**2** Click Free Trial, then select Limited Membership (free)

**3** To register, you provide your name, email address, password, location and phone number

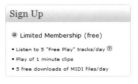

**4** Click Create Membership to set up your account. You'll be warned if the email address you specify is already in use

---

**Hot tip**

Members, registered free, can play up to five pieces per day (which could include multiple tracks), download up to five Midi files, and play short segments of any recording.

---

**Hot tip**

No payment is needed, and no credit card details are asked for, or required.

...cont'd

As a free member, you can purchase and download an MP3 version of any recording. Full members get a 10% discount.

**5** An email is sent to the address you specify, but your membership is activated immediately – no need to respond to the email

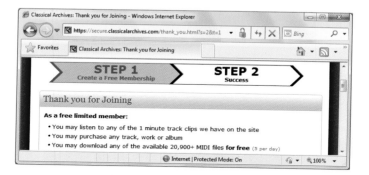

**6** Select Composers or Artists and you can choose free tracks from the recordings available

**7** Click Home to select one of the free concerts, offered as classical introductions

**8** Click Free 1-Click Concert to play the tracks in your default player, for example Windows Media Player

You can upgrade your membership to allow unlimited play, on a 14 day trial or for a monthly fee of $9.95.

**9** Go to www.classicalarchives.com/radio to listen to continuous classical music on Internet radio

# 6 Arts and Crafts

*Whether you want to view pictures and drawings by contemporary artists or by old masters, or get help and advice for creating your own works of art, the Internet has information, and a host of tutorials, to help you improve your skills.*

# Web Gallery of Art

The Web Gallery of Art is a virtual museum, and searchable database, of European painting and sculpture:

**1** Go to the website www.wga.hu and click Enter Here

**2** Type the artist and the title (e.g. Vermeer, Girl with Pearl Earring) and the date or format, if known, then press Search to find matching pictures

**3** Click the preview image to see the picture, or detail, full size. Click the Info button for comments and reviews

# Visit the Sistine Chapel

To see the features of the Web Gallery of Art in action, it is useful to take one of the predefined guided tours.

**1** Click the Tours button and select the tour you wish to take, for example a visit to the Sistine Chapel in the Vatican

**2** Click Start, then select a section of the tour to see detailed images and instructive comments

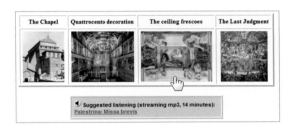

**3** Some sections may be further subdivided, so you can explore in greater detail. For example, you can zoom in to view the Sistine Chapel ceiling close up

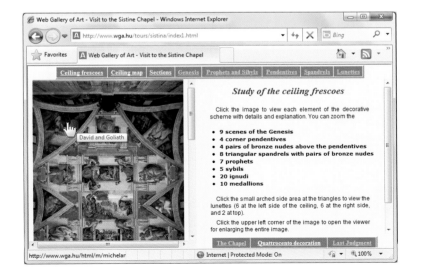

**Don't forget**

There are 16 different guided tours defined on the website.

**Hot tip**

Appropriate music to accompany the tour is suggested, in the form of a streaming MP3 that runs through Windows Media Player.

**Hot tip**

This tour shows how you can click parts of the image to zoom in and see details and explanations. Other tours demonstrate more facilities, such as dual mode (side by side) presentations.

# Water Color Painting

If you are interested in learning to paint in water color, or want to develop your skill, there are websites to help you.

**1** At www.watercolorpainting.com there are tutorials, step by step guides and lots of art related links

### Don't forget

Hold down Shift and Ctrl as you click the Tutorials link, to open it in a new IE tab, then switch to that tab.

**2** Click the Tutorials tab for an introduction to water color painting, and for basic or advanced tutorials

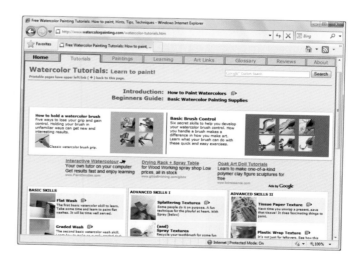

**3** Click Paintings for step by step painting guides, explaining the materials and techniques used

# Learn to Draw

Perhaps you've always wanted to draw, but never had the time. Now may be just the time to begin.

**1** Search for the phrase, learn to draw, for a list of websites related to this topic

**2** Select www.learn-to-draw.com, to get sets of easy to follow instructions for a variety of drawing tasks

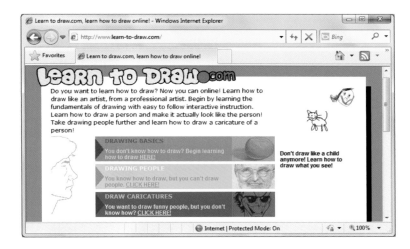

**3** Pick the tutorial that suits your existing skill level or interest

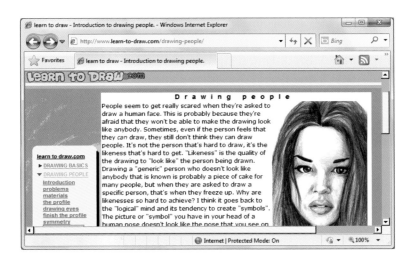

**Don't forget**

There will certainly be many websites offered. Some are purely for profit, some are there just to share an interest, while others turn out to be a mixture of both.

**Beware**

The Drawing Basics instructions are free, but the later topics, in Drawing People and Draw Caricatures, are available only to subscribers (who pay a one-time $16.95 fee).

# Pen and Ink Drawing

There's a step-by-step tutorial available on the Virtual Portmeirion website that tells you how to produce pen and ink drawings based on photographs.

**Hot tip**

Virtual Portmeirion is the site devoted to the village in North Wales created by Sir Clough Williams-Ellis, which has a collection of architectural follies in a variety of styles.

**88**

**Don't forget**

The tutorial uses Gates McFadden (Dr. Crusher in Star Trek) for its illustrations. You, of course, can use any photo you wish, but choose one that's sharp, since you'll be making a 10" or 12" digital enlargement.

**1** Visit www.virtualportmeirion.com/howto/ to see the list of steps involved in creating the drawing

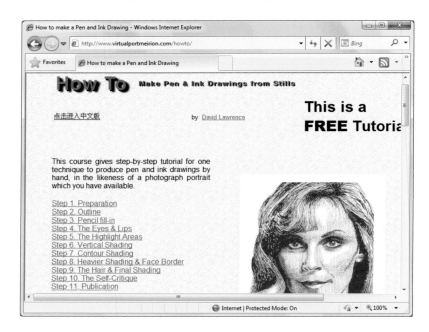

**2** You will need some suitable drawing tools:
- An extra fine black rolling ball pen
- A black felt tip pen
- A black broad tip magic marker
- A regular HB grade pencil
- A blue leaded pencil (blue doesn't photocopy)

**3** Each step contains detailed advice, with lots of useful tips and illustrative sketches. For example, in step 4 you learn how to draw eyes with reflective areas, positioned so that the subject is looking in the right direction

1

2

3

4

5

# Origami

What will you do with all that paper from your painting and drawing practice? Origami, the art of paper folding, sounds like the natural thing to try next.

**1** As usual, search for related sites by typing keywords, such as origami basic folds, into the Search box

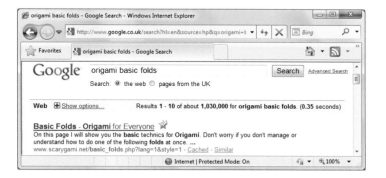

**Hot tip**

The Google search results may include images, such as Origami diagrams, as well as relevant web pages (1 million in this example).

**2** Go to www.scarygami.net/basic_folds.php to see the basic folds and to learn origami terms

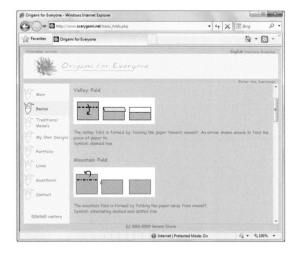

**Hot tip**

The Origami Basics also explain base figures, the starting points for many models, and there are diagrams for some traditional models, such as the Crane bird.

The Traditional Crane

**3** For projects, visit www.origami.com, where you'll find more than 400 models, with clear diagrams in Adobe .pdf format

# Celtic Knots

Celtic knots are motifs created by loops or continuous threads. They can be found on ancient stonework and in illuminated manuscripts, and in the form of jewelry and tattoos. You can also design and draw them on paper.

**1** Go to www.aon-celtic.com, click the Knotwork link, then click the Basic Celtic Knotwork tutorial

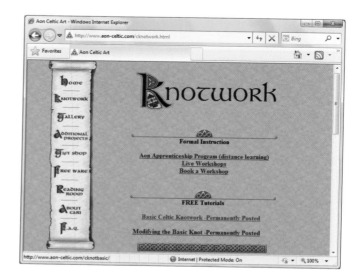

**2** Follow the steps in the tutorial to mark up a piece of graph paper, joining the sections and the corners, then deleting lines where threads overlap

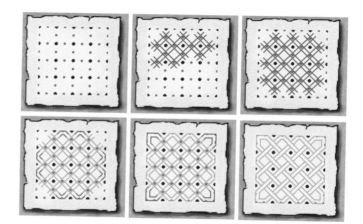

**Beware**

Associations, such as Love, Loyalty or Friendship, assigned to Celtic knot designs are inventions. The spiritual meanings of ancient symbols have been lost, while more recent symbols are merely decorative.

**Don't forget**

This website adds a new tutorial each month, covering different types of Celtic knots, to encourage repeat visits.

## ...cont'd

You can draw Celtic knots in your browser, with the help of applications provided on the Internet.

**3** Go to www.bit-101.com/celticknots and click Draw to generate the Celtic knot, as defined by the settings

**4** Click on the cross-overs, or adjacent segments, to change the ways they are connected

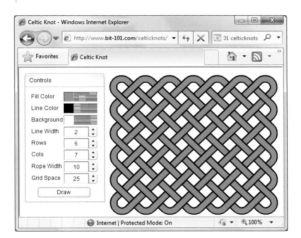

**5** Visit www.stevenabbott.co.uk/Knots/knots.html where you can download software to generate your own Celtic knot patterns

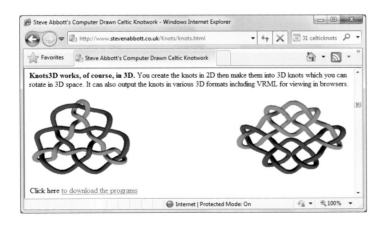

**Don't forget**

Drag the color sliders to change settings for Fill, Line and Background colors.

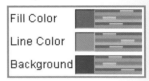

You can also set line width, number of rows and columns, rope width and grid space.

**Beware**

You must put a capital K in /Knots/ in this website address.

**Hot tip**

You must download and install version 3.42a first, then the latest version – 3.44k. You will then be able to run either version. You create the knots in 2D and turn them into 3D, which you can rotate in space.

# Cross Stitch

If your preference is for textiles and threads, you can find tutorials and patterns galore. These are often free of charge, even on websites that are online shops.

1. Visit the site www. birdcrossstitch.com to display the free cross stitch patterns offered

2. Click on the image to display links for the pattern sheets

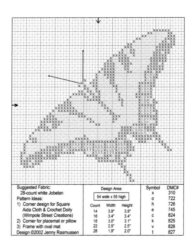

3. The patterns specify the positions and suggest the most suitable colors for the stitches. Instructions also indicate the finished size, using varying thread counts

If you are new to cross stitch, a tutorial will help. Many cross stitch websites reference the very comprehensive tutorial written by Kathleen Dyer. To view a copy:

**1** Go to home.comcast.net/~kathydyer/index.html and click the Counted Cross Stitch Tutorial link

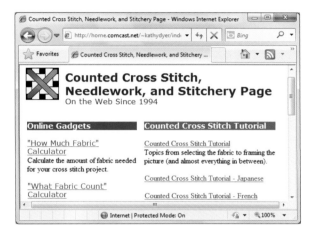

**2** The tutorial at www.celticxstitch.ie/learnhow.html offers a more graphical approach

**3** They advise using a kit, but they do tell you how to select your own materials

**Hot tip**

The Celtic X-stitch tutorial has animated illustrations of the single, block and back stitches used for cross stitching.

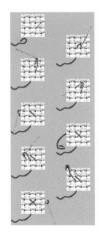

# Knitting

If you enjoy knitting and like to make items for charitable causes, you'll find inspiration at websites like Knitting Patterns Central at www.knittingpatternscentral.com.

**Hot tip**

The Free Pattern Directory lists about sixty categories, including afghans, bookmarks, coasters, hats, ponchos, teddy bears and toys, with numerous patterns in each.

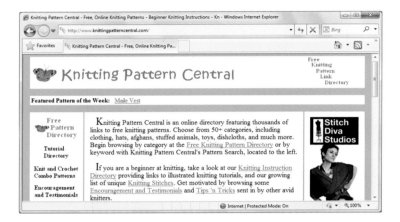

**Beware**

Some patterns are in PDF format (*), and some patterns require registration before viewing (+).

- *Bookmark Leandra
- +Bookmark Pen Holder
- Diamond Lace Bookmark

 **1** Select the pattern you want to review, for example the Diamond Lace Bookmark

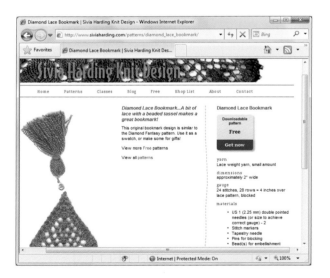

**Hot tip**

There are patterns available for all experience levels, and the website also provides a directory of instructions and tutorials for knitting techniques.

**2** This gives details of the materials, full instructions for knitting and finishing, and permission to use the pattern for personal or charity purposes only

# Guilds and Associations

Guilds and associations help you contact like-minded people, over the Internet or in local meetings.

**1** Visit the Knitting Guild Association (TKGA) website at www.tkga.com and click Guilds/Clubs

**2** Select Find a Local Guild/Club and specify your city or state (e.g. Kansas) to obtain a list for your area

**3** The guilds and clubs affiliated with TKGA in your area are listed, with the available contact details

# Other Crafts

If we haven't covered your favorite craft, search on Google, or explore a website, such as www.about.com, that provides preselected links for particular subjects.

1 Select a Channel (category), such as Hobbies & Games, and then a Topic, such as Woodworking, which is in the Arts/Crafts subcategory

2 Alternatively, the website www.allfiberarts.com covers many textile handicrafts, including crochet, dyeing, felting, knitting, sewing, spinning and weaving

# 7 Travel Plans

The Internet provides you with the tools available to travel agents, so you can search for suitable deals, compare prices offered by different services, and create your own custom holiday. The Internet tells you what's going on at your chosen destination, and gives you maps to help you find your way there.

### Don't forget

People over 50 make up the majority of travelers worldwide. They have the time and the freedom to travel, and, with the help of the Internet, can find options to match their interests and budgets.

### Hot tip

Which are the best websites for travel? Each will have its own particular strengths, so it all depends on what aspects you consider are important, how much of the work you are ready and able to do for yourself, and what time you have available for planning.

# World Wide Travel

There's a whole wide world of travel options available to you when you start planning a trip. You could be seeking a low cost holiday, or have a luxury holiday in mind. You might have plenty of time for research, or it could be a last-minute trip. Safety and comfort could be your key consideration, or you might be seeking adventure.

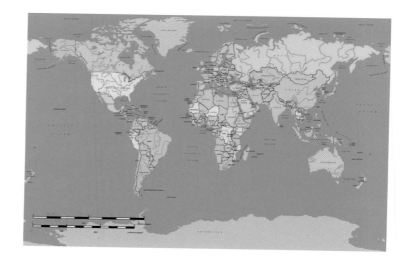

Whatever your requirements, the World Wide Web can help. There are many websites on the Internet devoted to one or more of the various aspects of travel, including:

- Transportation – air, sea, rail, road and river

- Accommodation – hotel, motel, b&b, self catering apartment, recreational vehicle, tent, camp site

- Destinations – domestic, overseas, remote location, single center, multicenter, tour, cruise

- Activities – sun and sand, sight seeing, city break, educational, cultural, sport, adventure, volunteer

- Information – maps, directions, guides, reviews, travel books, Internet access

- Facilities – itineraries, luggage, disabled suitability, currency, passports, adapters

# Online Travel Agents

The most natural choice, when you first start planning holidays on the Internet, is to use the online equivalent of the high street travel agent. There are a number of such websites, but Expedia is a popular choice.

1. Go to www.expedia.com (or the version for your location) to research, plan and purchase your trip

2. Select Sign In and, on your initial visit, click Create an Account. Fill in your name, email address and password, then click Create Expedia Account

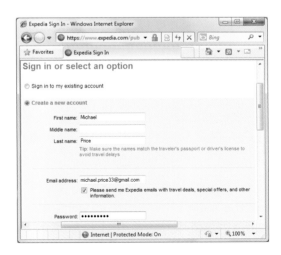

Beware

You can only purchase tickets and holidays from the version of the website meant for your home location, i.e. www.expedia.

| | |
|---|---|
| com | USA |
| au | Australia |
| ca | Canada |
| fr | France |
| de | Germany |
| it | Italy |
| nl | Netherlands |
| co.uk | UK |

Don't forget

Enter your first name and surname exactly as they appear on your passport.

Hot tip

You must accept the terms and conditions before you can create an Expedia account.

# Book Flights

Most travel plans start with the flights, since these are often the limiting factor, due to their cost or the availability of seats.

**Don't forget**

Click the date box to display a calendar, and select the desired date. Specify My dates are flexible if appropriate.

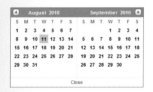

**1** At www.expedia.com, select Flight only, and then enter the Departing From city and Going To city

**2** Set the departing and returning dates and times, and select the number and type of passengers

**3** Click Search for Flights to look for round trips between the selected cities, on the specified dates and times

**Don't forget**

Click the down-arrow next to the city to see a list of airports, and their distance from the city centre, and select a specific airport.

**4** Refine the search by specifying particular airports, or airlines, change the class of ticket, or choose direct (nonstop) or refundable flights

For example, you could select New York (JFK) and
Vancouver (YVR), and request direct flights with Delta, to
produce a shortlist of options:

**Don't forget**

You can View flights
separately, to select
the departure flight
and the return flight
individually, or View
complete roundtrips.

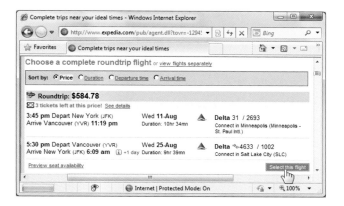

**1**   Review the flights offered, then click Choose this
flight for the roundtrip that you wish to book

**2**   Review flight details, and the rules and restrictions
that apply, e.g. This fare is nonrefundable

**Hot tip**

You may be offered
the chance to add a
hotel or a rental car
to your booking. Then
you can choose to
purchase, reserve, save
or cancel the booking.

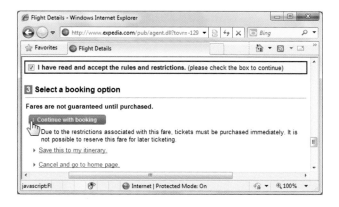

**3**   Select to Continue with Booking and provide
payment details, or choose Save this to my itinerary
for later. Alternatively, click Cancel and go to home
page, to discard the suggestions

**Hot tip**

The tickets are not
purchased, and
the fares are not
guaranteed, until you
have supplied your
credit card details and
confirmed the order.

# Book Your Hotel

You can choose to book your hotel rooms while you are purchasing your flight tickets, or you can treat this as a separate transaction.

**1** At www.expedia.com, select Hotel only, then enter the Destination city or airport, e.g. Vancouver

**2** Set the check-in and the check-out dates, then select the number of rooms, and the number of adults and children

**3** Click Search for hotels to list the hotels near your destination

**4** You can specify preferences to limit the list, and you can also see the hotels on a map

**Hot tip**

Zoom in and pan to the area that interests you, then click Update hotels on map.

**5** Select the hotel that best suits your needs, then click to make the order (or save to your itinerary)

## Booking Direct

If you regularly stay with a particular chain of hotels, you may prefer to book direct. For example, to choose a hotel from the Intercontinental chain (Holiday Inn etc), go to www.ichotelsgroup.com and specify your requirements.

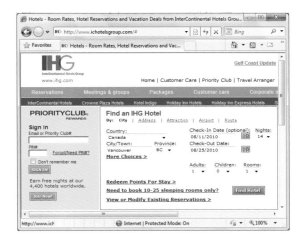

**Hot tip**

You might choose to book directly with Intercontinental, if you join their Priority Club Rewards scheme (see page 106). Other hotels have similar schemes.

# Book a Rental Car

You can book a rental car along with your flight tickets, or in a separate transaction.

**1** At www.expedia.com, select Car only, then the Pick-up location and the Car type

**2** Choose the pick-up and the drop-off dates and times, and click the Search for Cars button

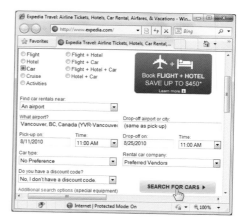

The cars are displayed in price bands, but you can display them by car size or car hire company.

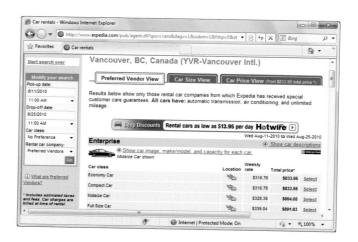

**3** Click Select to see the full details for a particular car. Charges are shown in your home currency

**4** Continue the booking to confirm the driver details and book the car, or save the details in your itinerary

➡ **Continue with booking.**
➡ Save this to my itinerary.
➡ Cancel and go to the home page.

# Other Online Travel Agents

Like Expedia, the www.travelocity.com website helps you book flights, hotels, cars, package holidays and cruises.

Hot tip

If you have the time, run the same travel query on several of the travel agent websites and explore the differences.

Orbitz at www.orbitz.com, set up by a group of American airlines but now independently owned, offers similar services.

Hot tip

If you book a flight or prepaid hotel room on Orbitz and another customer books the same itinerary at a lower price, Orbitz will issue a refund for the difference, automatically.

If you are in Europe, visit Opodo at www.opodo.com and select the country you are travelling in, to try local options

# Loyalty Cards

Airlines operate programs to encourage travellers to stay loyal to the particular airline, or alliance of airlines. For example, American Airlines operates its own AAdvantage program and participates in the OneWorld program, with British Airways, Cathay Pacific, Qantas and other airlines.

Hotels also offer loyalty programs, which earn miles (in collaboration with airline programs) or points, that can be exchanged for accommodation or other goods and services.

Car rental companies also offer loyalty programs, which can be linked to various hotel and airline loyalty programs.

**Beware**

Keep track of the members of an alliance, since they may change.

**Don't forget**

Some online booking options may exclude loyalty cards and points, or may offer their own alternatives, such as Nectar points at Expedia, so take this into account when choosing an option.

**Hot tip**

All loyalty programs include elite levels, such as silver or gold, awarded when you attain a certain number of air miles or points during the membership year.

# Last-Minute Bookings

Last-minute booking is perhaps the complete antithesis of loyalty programs – you have to take whatever you can get.

1. Visit website www.priceline.com, and enter your journey details for a roundtrip or one way journey

2. Click Search Now to list flights available from a variety of airlines

3. Choose your preferred option from the lowest price flights or the non-stop flights

Hot tip

If you are flexible on dates, and will fly any time of day, use any major airline, stay in any name-brand hotel and rent from any car rental agency, you might be able to save a lot of money.

Beware

Prices may rise, even if you are in the middle of confirming the offer. However, you won't be obliged to complete the transaction.

# Name Your Own Price

With Priceline, you can make a bid for a flight, with your requirements and the price you are willing to pay, and see if any supplier is willing to accept it.

**Don't forget**

Since you provide the price, not the supplier, this is known as a reverse auction.

**1** Search flights at www.priceline.com, and select Start Here to name your own price

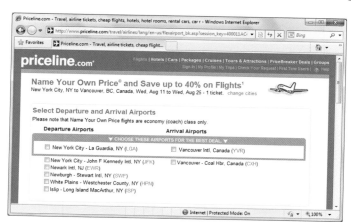

**2** Confirm the departure and arrival airports to be used

**Hot tip**

If you specify too low a figure, you'll be told the published fare and taxes, and recommended to raise your offer to 40% discount or even 20-30% discount.

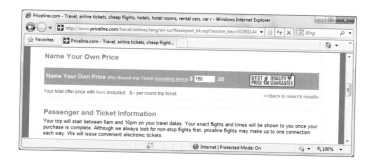

**3** Specify your total offer, with fees included

**Beware**

If an airline accepts your price, tickets will be purchased. These will be non-refundable, non-transferable and non-changeable. They are not eligible for frequent flyer miles.

**4** Provide passenger details, billing address and credit card number, then click Buy my rickets now

**5** Await a response to your request for the flight

# Travel Guide

To help you explore your destination and surroundings, you need a travel guide that will tell everything you need to know, laid out in a clear and consistent format.

**1** Go to www.mytravelguide.com and Search for your destination, e.g. Christchurch, New Zealand

**2** The guide gives details, such as hotels, attractions, restaurants and nearby towns, for the specified city

**3** Select the city map link and click the map for a detailed street plan

## Hot tip

MyTravelGuide lists related destinations, so you can select the most appropriate one.

## Don't forget

MyTravelGuide is owned by Priceline, but it is completely free to use, and covers locations worldwide. If you register, you can create quick links and save your itineraries.

# Google Maps

For an alternative map of your destination and surroundings:

**1** Open the Google website and select Maps

**2** Enter the place you are seeking, for example Christchurch, New Zealand, and click Search Maps

**3** The street plan of Christchurch is displayed, based on Cathedral Square, which is the city centre

**110**

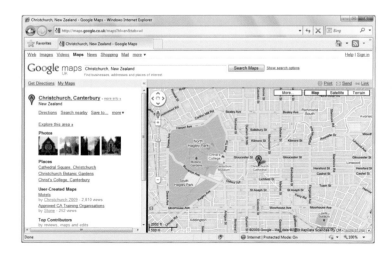

**4** Click the Satellite button to get a bird's eye view

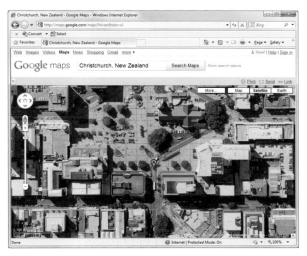

**5** Click and drag the Pegman icon onto the street map to get a panoramic view of the location

**6** Drag the picture to move along, or re-orientate the view (360° horizontally, 270° vertically).

# Plan a Road Trip

If you are planning a driving holiday, Google Maps can provide directions, and does allow intermediate destinations. However, you might prefer a dedicated route planner.

**1** For trips around Canada and the USA visit the website www.randmcnally.com and click Road Explorers

**2** For Europe, Australia and New Zealand, you can go to www.multimap.com and select Directions

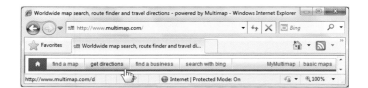

**112**

**3** Enter the starting address, city/town or postcode, click Find and select from the locations suggested

**4** Put the destination point details next, again selecting from the suggested list, if necessary

**Hot tip**

The route planner can handle routes that include a ferry trip, as one will be required between North Island and South Island in New Zealand.

**5** Click Go Via, and add intermediate points (up to ten points in total) to complete the route

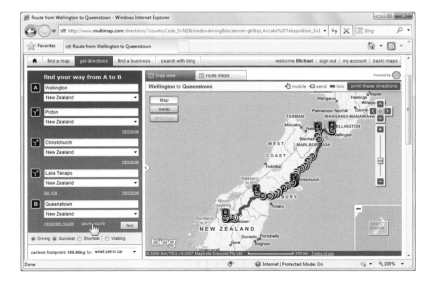

**Don't forget**

Click the Map View tab to see the large map of the route, or click Route Steps to see the detailed directions.

113

**6** Select Save File, then Confirm to save the route in your Favorite routes & places

# Print Trip Guide

When you have completed and saved the route, you can view, edit, or print the trip whenever you wish.

**1** At www.multimap.com, click MyMultimap to log in, then select Get Directions

**2** Select the trip from Favorite routes & places

**3** Click Print These Directions

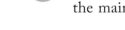

**4** Choose Print Standard for directions with maps of the main and intermediate destinations

**5** Choose Print Detailed for an overview map, plus mini-map, showing the whole trip turn by turn

**6** Click the Print button to select your printer and print out the journey plan

# Traffic Reports

For a road trip, a key factor will be the traffic situation. There are numerous websites devoted to this, no matter where you are travelling. For the United States and Canada:

**1** Go to www.highwayconditions.com and select the state or province where you will be travelling

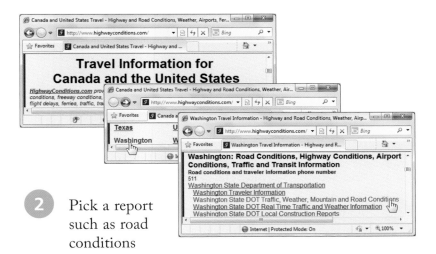

**2** Pick a report such as road conditions

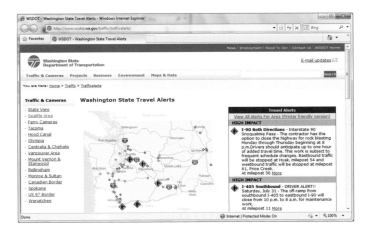

**3** Zoom to view more routes with problems reported

**4** Select a Traffic & Cameras area such as Seattle for the detailed traffic status

For the UK, Frixo.com gives live traffic news and information, with details of delays and incidents that may affect your journey.

Don't forget

This map identifies current incidents and classifies them according to type and level, so you can judge the likely effect on your journey.

# Weather Reports

Whatever method of travel you use for your journey, up to date information about the weather will be important. Again, the Internet is a ready source. For example:

**1** Go to www.weather.com and enter the zip, city or place for which you'd like a current weather report

**2** For other countries, scroll to the bottom and select International Sites

**3** Enter the city name, and select the required city from the list

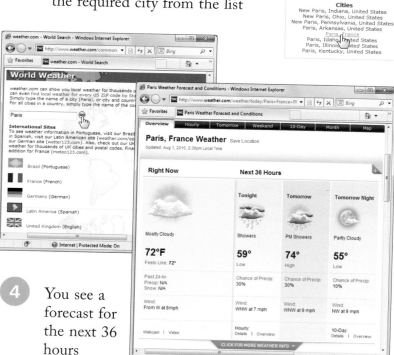

**4** You see a forecast for the next 36 hours

# 8 Explore Your Family Tree

The Internet has created a whole new way to search for information on your family background and your ancestors. You can share information with other parts of the same family, without having to travel around, even if your ancestral roots are from far distant shores.

# Introduction to Genealogy

The term Genealogy applies to the study of the history of past and present members of a particular family. It also applies to the records and documentation that describe that history, the members of the family, and their relationships.

Genealogy is highly popular right across the world. There are many reasons why you might research your family's history:

● Simple curiosity about yourself and your roots

● Making your children aware of their ancestors

● Preserve family cultural and ethnic traditions

● Family medical history (inherited disease or attribute)

● Join a lineage or heritage society

Getting started is generally quite easy – you find the oldest living members of your family and ask them about other members, especially those who are no longer here to answer for themselves.

After the first flush of success, however, it could become difficult to fill in the gaps and extend the history further back in time. You have to rely on official records, and this could require a lot of travel, especially if your family originated overseas. Fortunately, much of the necessary legwork can now be accomplished over the Internet, there's plenty of advice and guidance, and you'll be able to capitalize on the research that others have carried out.

The information you glean can be recorded on charts designed to organize genealogical data.

● Ascendant, Ahnentafel and Pedigree charts

● Descendant, Progenitor charts

● Family Group sheets

These forms, and the way to use them, are described in various tutorials (see page 121).

**Don't forget**

Other equivalent terms are ancestry, forebears, descent, lineage and pedigree, though that last term is usually associated with non-human groupings.

**Beware**

Genealogy research can turn into an obsession, as you reach further back in time to solve puzzles and discover facts that others have missed.

**Hot tip**

You can download versions of these forms to print and complete manually, or to fill out using your computer software (see details on page 121).

# Researching Your Family Tree

If you are new to genealogy, perhaps the best place to start is with an online (and free) genealogy tutorial.

**1** There's a tutorial on Researching Your Family Tree at www.learnwebskills.com/family/intro.html which provides a self-paced introduction

Hot tip

Search Google for "Genealogy Tutorial" (the quotes mean the exact phrase), and you get 7,350 matching web pages.

Hot tip

The navigation bar on the left lists the contents of the six modules, plus more than 20 useful website links.

**2** Follow the modules in this tutorial to research your own ancestors while learning to use the genealogical charts, online databases and other resources

**3** You can share ideas and issues with other users of the tutorial, through the Yahoo group known as Learngen. The tutorial website includes instructions for joining this group

Don't forget

The Tools section of the navigation bar has links to charts (see page 121).

**Tools**
Home Sources Checklist
5-Generation Ancestor Chart
4-Generation Ancestor Chart
Family Group Sheet
Birth Date Calculator
Town to County Database

# About Genealogy

**1** For a somewhat more structured introduction, go to genealogy.about.com and scroll to the Topics section

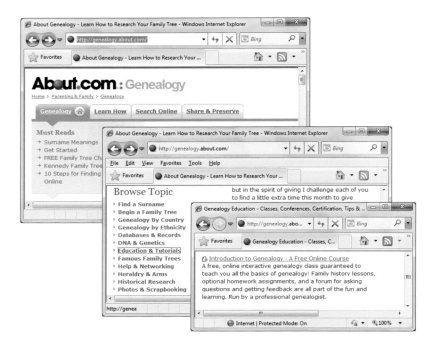

**2** Select Education & Tutorials and scroll down to Introduction to Genealogy, a free online course

This class consists of four lessons:

- Genealogical Basics
- Family & Home Sources
- Genealogy Research 101
- Vital Records – Birth, Marriage, Death, Divorce

# Genealogy Charts

**1** Go to the website www.ancestry.com, click Learning Center, and select Build a tree

**Don't forget**

Most genealogy websites will have free charts available. There are also many commercial products on offer.

**2** Scroll to the Free Forms and Charts and select any entry

**3** Choose a form, for example Ancestral Chart, and click Download Form

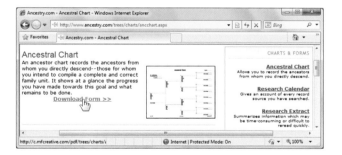

**Don't forget**

Right-click the link and select Save target as, to save a copy of the PDF file onto your hard drive (or click the Diskette icon in the browser view).

**4** You can view or print the PDF form in your browser

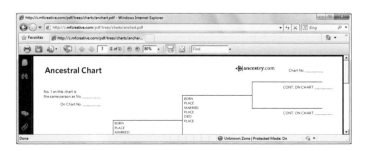

**Hot tip**

The Ancestry.com family tree resources also include a family group form, census forms for the US, UK and Canada, and other record forms.

# Charts in Text Format

If you want to complete your genealogy forms on your computer, you need the forms in a text format.

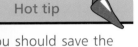 At the website www.familytreemagazine.com, click Research Toolkit and then Free Forms

## Hot tip

You should save the text file to disk, then right-click the file and choose your word processor to open it.

 Select a group of forms, then click PDF for a particular form, to display it in the browser

Click Text to download the form as a Word file

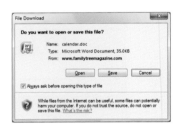

## Beware

The two versions of the forms are not identical, but the Word form does allow you to amend and append the layout and content on your PC, rather than manually.

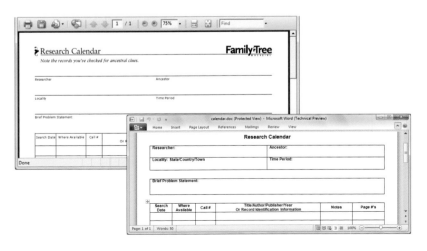

# Vital Records

When you've collected all the information you can from family members, and organized it using genealogy charts, you'll have a list of unanswered questions, and you'll need to start searching records to find some of the answers.

There are two main types of genealogical records that you can investigate:

### Original records

An original record is an account of a specific event, written at or near the time the event took place. Historically, many civil and religious authorities kept records on events in the lives of people in their jurisdictions. Original records include:

- Vital Records (birth, marriage, divorce and death)
- Church Records (christenings, baptisms, confirmations, marriages, or burials)
- Cemetery Records (names, dates and relationships)
- Census Records (household member name, sex, age, country or state of birth, occupation)
- Military, Probate, Immigration Records

### Compiled records

A compiled record is a collection of information on a specific person, family group or topic. Compiled records exist because others have already researched original records, or collated information from other compiled records, or other sources. Compiled records include:

- Ancestral File (over 35 million names, linked into ancestors and descendants)
- International Genealogical Index (computerized index of about 250 million names extracted from birth, christening, marriage, and other records)
- Published Family Histories, Biographies, Genealogies, and Local Histories

**Hot tip**

You may be able to access original records on microfiche, and some, especially census records, have been indexed and computerized.

**Don't forget**

Compiled records are useful if you want to learn about ancestors who were born before 1900, but are not likely to have information about modern families.

**Hot tip**

The two main compiled record files were developed by the family history department of the Church of Latter-Day Saints (see page 125).

# Cyndi's List

To find out where to look for original records, you should start at www.cyndislist.com, a search engine that is dedicated to genealogical research via the Internet. You can search for helpful websites by location, or by record type.

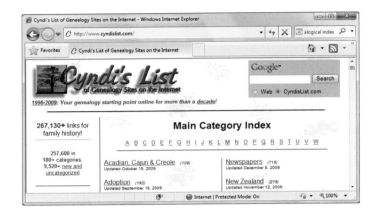

**1** Click Beginners in the main category index, and you'll be able to view lists of websites related to researching various types of original and vital records

**2** Researching: Census Records gives lists of USA and worldwide census sites, plus details on Soundex indexing of surnames

# FamilySearch

The www.familysearch.org website, owned and operated by the Church of Latter-day Saints, provides free family history.

**Don't forget**

Advanced Search lets you add parent and spouse names for a particular ancestor.

1. The minimum information you need to provide is the surname. The exact spelling isn't essential

2. Select a record type (life event) for which you have the year (exact, or give or take 2, 5, 10 or 20 years)

3. Choose the country (and the state or province, for the United States and Canada)

4. The matching records are displayed for review

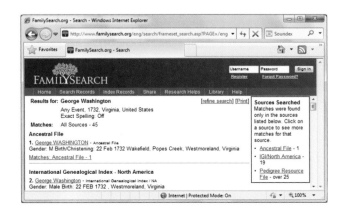

**Hot tip**

The individual records will provide you with further clues about the person, perhaps including, as in this case, pedigree charts, family group records and further links.

# Ancestry.com

You can search for ancestors at www.ancestry.com. This website has many databases, including census, birth, marriage, death, military and immigration. It offers paid membership subscriptions, but there is a free Registered Guest account, which allows you to receive the free newsletter and build an online family tree, and access to some of the databases.

**1** To register for a Guest account, select Help and type Guest in the Keyword box, then click the Search button

**2** Select the search result Ancestry Guest Registration to find the Overview, where you can select Click Here to create a guest account

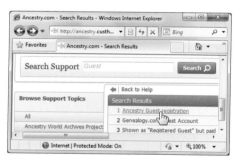

**Overview of Guest registration**

To use any of the features on Ancestry, a user must have at least a Guest registration. To create a registered guest account, click here. As a Registered Guest, a limited number of resources are available at no cost. These can be created by providing a first and last name and an email address.

**3** Register your details, and your guest user name and password will be displayed

**4** Search for one of your ancestors, giving all the details that you have available

**5** Click Tell Us More, for parents and spouse, etc

**6** The Categories with related entries are listed

**7** Select a category such as Census & Voters lists

**8** Choose a relevant list, e.g. Virginia Census, to see the matching records

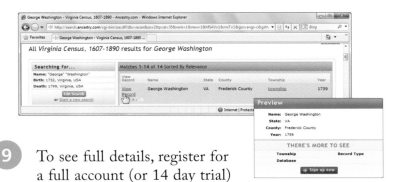

**9** To see full details, register for a full account (or 14 day trial)

# US National Archives

Some of the answers to your questions may be found in the US National Archives, at www.archives.gov.

**1** Select the Genealogists/Family Historians link where you'll find help and guidance to get started

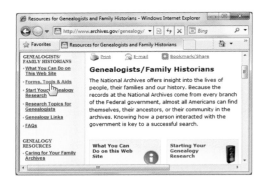

**2** Select Forms, Tools & Aids, which includes help to order records online, links to other resources and guidance to hire an independent researcher

**3** You can visit one of the National Archives centers in person for some of your research

# Other National Archives

Other countries will have their own national archives. For Australian information, go to www.naa.gov.au, then, under Using the Archives, click Family history.

Hot tip

Any person is entitled to visit the archives and use the services. It isn't necessary to be an Australian citizen or resident.

You'd visit www.collectionscanada.ca for Canadian records, and select Genealogy and Family History.

Don't forget

When you visit the Canadian website, you must select the English or French version.

The UK has its records at www.nationalarchives.gov.uk. You'd select Records, In-depth Research Guides and then locate the Family History guides in the alphabetic index.

Hot tip

There are around 300 in-depth guides on the UK National Archives website, to help you with your research.

# Immigrant Records

If parts of your family are from overseas, you will need to find the connection between the family groups. Immigration records may be the answer.

In the USA, the website www.immigrantships.net makes passenger lists available from a number of ships.

After 1820, the federal government required passenger lists from ship captains. You will find earlier records at www.genealogy.com.

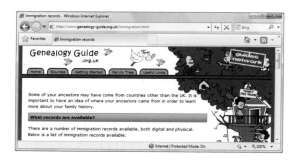

Ellis Island, just off Manhattan Island, New York, became the gateway to the United States from 1892 to 1924, for over 20 million immigrants. See website www.ellisisland.org.

The main website at genealogy-guide.org.uk has information about many sources of family history records.

For information about UK immigration records, go to the website www.genealogy-guide.org.uk/immigration.html.

# 9 Digital Photography

*Find advice and guidance on the Internet to improve your skill and technique. Store and backup your digital photographs, and print online photos. Share your photos with your friends and family, and view the results obtained from using various cameras and lenses.*

# Tips on the Internet

To help you get started, there are websites that tell you how to improve your digital photography skills and techniques.

 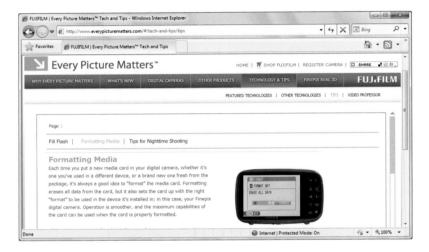
**1** Fuji has some tips for better photographs at the website www.everypicturematters.com. Select Technology & Tips, then select Tips, then choose a tip

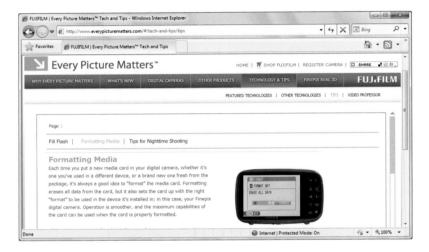

**132**

**2** There's a more comprehensive website offered by Kodak. Go to www.kodak.com and select the button for Tips & Projects Center

**3** Review all the entries in the sections Learn, Create, Tips from the Pros, and Inspirational Photo Stories. You can also view the Picture of the Day (or submit your own entry)

# Tutorials

There are numerous tutorials on various aspects of digital photography, some for beginners, for example those at the ShortCourses website:

**1** Switch to www.shortcourses.com/workflow for a short course on digital photography workflow

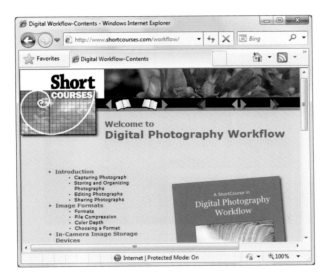

**2** If you are ready for a challenge, view the tutorial Making fine prints in your digital darkroom, at the www.normankoren.com website

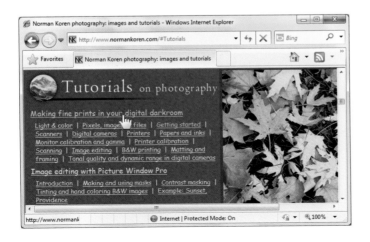

**Hot tip**

Click the Home page link to see the full list of the short courses that are on offer. You can view them freely online, or download a PDF version (for a fee).

**Don't forget**

Click the Tutorials on Photography link (or add the #Tutorials bookmark to the website address) to display the list of tutorials.

**Hot tip**

This is a multi-part series that introduces tools and techniques for making fine prints digitally, to meet the highest aesthetic and technical standards.

# Find Inspiration

Digital photography is not just about equipment and techniques, it is also about subject and composition. Perhaps the best way to explore these aspects is through viewing the work of other photographers, for example at the Photographic Society of America.

**1** Visit www.psa-photo.org to see a series of examples. Click the Galleries link to select a gallery, and choose members by name to view their work

**2** The Royal Photographic Society allows members to upload their portfolios to the Society website. They can be viewed at www.rps.org/portfolios.php

# Share Photos Online

You can use the Internet to share your digital photographs. You don't have to join a society and create a portfolio, and the photographs can be private, just for friends and family.

**1** Visit www.ofoto.com and click to Join the gallery

**Hot tip**

Kodak runs Ofoto, so the address becomes www.kodakgallery.com, but you can use either address to visit the website.

**2** Enter your first name, email address and password

**3** Agree terms and conditions, accept offers and news if desired, and click Create. No credit card number is needed

**4** Your account will be assigned and you will receive an email message to confirm

**5** You can now upload and share your photographs

**Don't forget**

If you are located outside the US, click the Change link and select your country before registering, to get local prices and shipping charges.

# Upload Photographs

**1** Click Upload now to create your first album at Kodak Gallery

**2** Provide the album title, album date and a brief description, then click Browse to add pictures

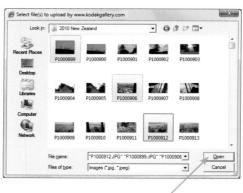

**3** Select photos and click Open to add them, then click Upload to transfer them

Upload

Upload Completed
30 of 30 successfully uploaded

# View Albums

**1** Sign in to Kodak Gallery (or click Photos if you are already signed in) to see your albums

**2** Click one of your albums to display thumbnails of its contents

137

**3** Click Slideshow to see larger copies of the photos. Click Done to end the show

**Hot tip**

Click Photo Options on a thumbnail to edit, share or download that photo.

**Don't forget**

Select Photo Options, Edit Photo to rotate, crop or adjust quality, Click Undo or Revert to original, to cancel changes.

# Share Albums

Invite your friends and family to view your photographs:

**1** Drag albums into the photo tray, or click the Select box for individual photos

**2** Review the contents of the photo tray, to remove photos that are not needed

**3** When you've added all the photos you want to share, click Share Photos

**4** Choose to share photos via Email

**5** Enter the email addresses, amend the subject as needed, then add your message and click Send

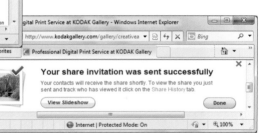

# View Friends' Albums

Similarly, your friends can invite you to share their albums, by sending you an email. To accept the invitation:

Beware

You and your friends could use Facebook to share photos, but this means Kodak security features won't apply. It is usually better to share via Email.

**1** Click the View Photos link in your email, and sign in to view your friend's slideshow

**2** When you click Done to exit the slideshow, you'll find the new album in the My Friends' Albums area

## Don't forget

You can treat the shared photos just like your own and share them with others or buy prints etc.

# Order Prints

Kodak provides a printing service, which is their motivation for providing storage on the Internet. They keep the original image file (even though slideshows use reduced images) so prints will be full quality.

**Hot tip**

You can add all the photos from the album in a single step. You can then remove individual photos that are not required.

**Hot tip**

As well as normal prints, you can order posters, collages, frames, greeting cards, stickers, cards and calendars, plus mugs, coasters and tote bags, all decorated with your photos.

**1** Sign in to your Kodak Gallery account and select photos you want to print, to add them to the photo tray

**2** When you've finished choosing photos, click Buy Prints

**3** Specify Quick Print Settings for photo size, paper quality, color management, borders and tints if required

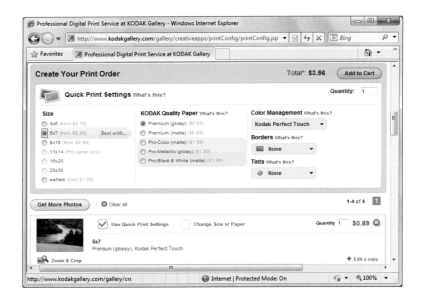

**4** You can use these settings for all the photos in your order, or specify settings for individual photos

**5** Click Add to Cart to continue the order process, when you have entered all your requirements

**6** Choose the shipping option and provide the delivery address details, then click Checkout

**Hot tip**

The first address entered becomes the default delivery address. If you add another recipient, you have the option to change the default.

**7** Provide your credit card details, Clear the box Save the card, if you don't want details kept

**Beware**

You will be charged prices and shipping based on the website where you register (see page 135). If you are US based, but have a UK account, you'll pay international shipping.

**8** Specify the billing address, or click Use a Shipping Address, to use an existing entry, then click Next

**9** Check the order and delivery details, then select Place Order to complete the purchase

**Don't forget**

You can click Clear Cart at any time to cancel the order. You aren't committed until you select Place Order.

# Storage Policy

To check the storage policy for your Kodak Gallery account:

**1** Sign in to Kodak Gallery and select My Account

**2** Select Your Storage Status

**3** Click Learn more, to see the full Terms of Service

The Kodak Gallery provides free online storage for an unlimited number of photos. However, to maintain free storage, you must make at least one purchase from the Gallery every 12 months. The purchase must amount to $4.99 for up to 2GB storage, or $19.99 for above 2GB storage.

# Yahoo Photos

There are other websites that offer free online photo storage, Flickr, for example. This requires you to have a Yahoo ID to sign up (see page 167 to create a free Yahoo ID).

**1** Go to www.flickr.com and click Create Your Account

**2** Sign in to Yahoo using your existing ID and password

**3** Choose your Flickr screen name, then click Create a new Account

**4** Click Personalize your profile, or Upload your first photo, or Find your friends on Flickr

Hot tip

With a free Flickr account, you can upload 100MB of photos per month. However, only the latest 200 photos can be viewed. Flickr is most useful for sharing pictures of events, such as a wedding or a celebration.

143

Don't forget

On Flickr, you can choose to make your photos private or public or make them available to groups of people with shared interests.

# PBase Galleries

The PBase photo sharing and hosting site encourages public viewing, giving serious photographers the opportunity to display their skills to the world. You'll usually find information on the settings and equipment used, and lots of comments made by other viewers.

**1** The PBase website is at www.pbase.com. Click Popular Galleries to view slideshows, or click the Search button to look for particular subjects

**2** For example, a search for Auroras produced several pages of fascinating Northern Lights slideshows

# 10 For the Grandchildren

*Here we look at sharing your computer with the grandchildren when they come to visit. You can give them their own user identity, control their web activities, and encourage safe web browsing. We look at websites that will enable you to help and educate them, while also entertaining them.*

# Create a User Account

To avoid problems that arise when you share your computer with others, especially children, give them their own User Account. Your own files and desktop settings will then remain secure, and cannot be affected or changed by their actions.

 Go to Start, Control Panel and select Add or remove user accounts, in the User Accounts and Family Safety section

**User Accounts and Family Safety**
Add or remove user accounts
Set up parental controls for any user

2 In the Manage Accounts window, select Create a new account

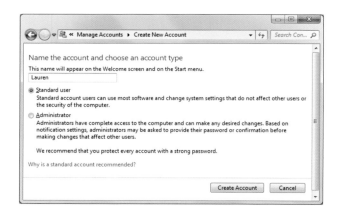

3 Choose Standard user, and click Create Account. The account will appear with an image automatically allocated

4 Double-click the new account and select Change the picture, to allow the child to select a personalized image

# Set Up Parental Controls

With the account now active, take the opportunity to manage which programs and games the child can access, and how much time can be spent on the computer.

**1** In User Accounts and Family Safety, choose Set up parental controls for any user

**2** Single click the child's account. You will be offered Windows Live Family Safety. Close this window for the moment, to view the Parental Controls included in Windows 7, as you may decide they are sufficient

**3** Turn Parental Controls on. You will now be able to create time limits, and control access to games and other programs

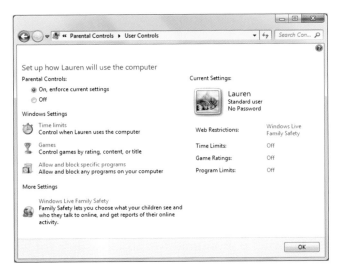

**4** Choose Time Limits to display a list where you can restrict use by day/hour blocking

**5** Access to Games is by rating. All games supplied with Windows 7 are rated acceptable to all users

**6** You may choose to block particular programs, such as Messenger, Skype, or even Internet Explorer

## Hot tip

Windows Live Family Safety offers a greater degree of safety and monitoring (see pages 148-9 for details).

## Don't forget

You could allow visiting children to use a Guest account, for short term access. This will prevent any changes to your own files and preferences, but does not allow you to apply parental controls.

## Hot tip

When you choose to block specific programs, you will be presented with the list of programs on your PC. You will have to use the Browse option to locate Internet Explorer and games you have added.

# Windows Live Family Safety

Windows Live Family Safety is included as part of Windows Live Essentials, and must be downloaded before use. It can be used to restrict access to undesirable websites, and to monitor computer usage for all users registered.

**1** Select Start and type Family Safety in the Search box, then click the link that appears. Sign in or register on the Family Safety website

**2** Users with their own Windows account will be listed. Select the account to monitor and click Save

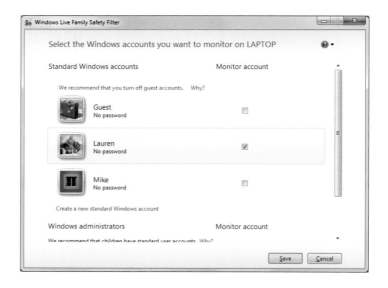

**3** You will be prompted to add passwords for accounts that are currently not password protected. Click the link to Add passwords, if required. Click Next

**4** In the Customize settings for your family, click the link to visit the Family Safety website

Customize settings for your family

Parents can approve or block websites and contacts, and get online activity reports on the Family Safety website.

Go to the Family Safety website: familysafety.live.com

**5** Family members will be listed and so will the computer on which they are registered. Click Edit settings for the new addition

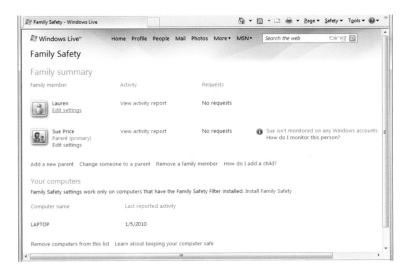

**6** Standard settings are for Web filtering Basic and Activity reporting On. Click on any of the settings links in the left column to make changes

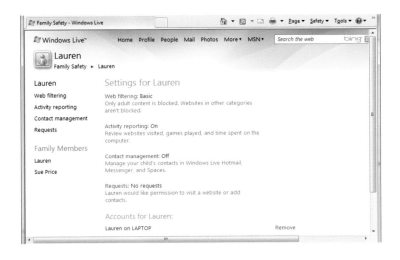

# Online Safety

The Think U Know website, at www.thinkuknow.com/, is an initiative created and managed by the Child Exploitation and Online Protection (CEOP) Centre. The site is co-sponsored by the EU and is a member of the Virtual Global Taskforce, who work to make the Internet a safer place.

The Think U Know website is designed to teach children, between the ages of 5 to 16, how to use the Internet and latest technology safely. Each age grouping uses a variety of appropriate methods.

The 5-7 age group introduces Hector, a friendly dolphin, to teach basic rules. The site offers a Safety Button which, when clicked, immediately covers the current screen.

1  Select the 5-7 group, click Hector's World and click the Hector's World Safety Button

2  Download and install the relevant version for your operating system

3  Open the Control Panel and click the link to Set up parental controls

**4** Select the user name for the child and, in the More settings area, click Hector's World Safety Button

**4** The next time the child logs on to the PC, they will see a small swimming dolphin. Click the dolphin to hide the current screen

Older children and teenagers will wish to be more adventurous with their Internet use, and may want to spend time on social networking sites. Whilst most sites have ways to report abuse, bullying, and inappropriate content, the Bebo site offers a direct link to the CEOPs site.

Google offers a SafeSearch feature to filter search results. Sign in using your Google account (see page 204). In Search Settings, select Lock the SafeSearch feature to screen out content you would prefer your children not to see. Colored balls on the screen indicate that SafeSearch is operating.

**Don't forget**

Parental Controls will be turned on, and Hector's World Safety Button will be activated for that child's user account.

Lauren
Standard user - Parental Controls On
No Password

**Hot tip**

The top three social networking sites are Facebook, MySpace and Bebo. Of these three, Bebo scores highest on its privacy settings. For more on Social Networking, see Chapter 13.

**Don't forget**

Search engines may generate links to inappropriate sites, unless you apply some form of filtering of the results.

# Early Learning

PBS provides a number of excellent websites for children. To entertain the youngest, visit www.pbskids.org/, where you'll find shows, games and videos targeted at the pre-school age.

The main list of activities uses a voice to introduce the topics, so even non-readers can select a program.

**1**   Move the mouse over the arrows to rotate the dial and move over a show icon to hear the title

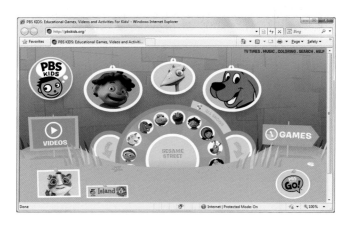

**2**   Select Sesame Street for games, videos, printables (coloring pages, bookmarks etc) and e-cards

**3**   Scroll down and play tunes on the hanging chimes, or click a chime to display that character

Encourage a degree of concentration with a program, such as some of those offered on the Nick Junior website at www.nickjr.com/games/index.jhtml, the home of Dora the Explorer, a children's favorite.

1　Open the website and scroll down the Game Finder column, where activities are arranged by Show, Theme and Age

2　Select Matching and Sorting and then a game, such as the Mermaid Matching Game

### Hot tip

Use the Game Finder column to help you set criteria for suitable games. For example, select Dora the Explorer, then Matching and Sorting, and apply an age range.

153

### Beware

The website is based in the US, and some of the video clips on the site are not able to be viewed outside of the United States.

3　The chosen game will indicate the developmental skills involved and the target age range. Games have voice direction and narration and make many encouraging comments

4　The site is commercial, although not overtly so. You are able to buy items from the shop or just sign up for a free newsletter

# Familiar Names

Children often prefer the familiar, so may welcome the opportunity to play and learn online with well known names from books they have read. For example, the Mr. Men official website at www.mrmen.com/us/ introduces all the Mr. Men (and Little Miss) characters by name.

 **1** Click on any character to open their particular web page, where you can choose their game. The games are different for each personality and require differing degrees of concentration and mouse skills

**2** Alternatively, children can watch a video involving the chosen character or select 'free stuff', which includes a downloadable image for use as desktop wallpaper

 **3** Older children will love the Pinball game. It uses the arrow keys to fire the ball and manage the paddles

Fisher-Price, the toy maker, offers activities for infant, toddler and preschool age children on their website at www.fisher-price.com/.

1. Select Games and Activities, Online Games to view the full range. The games are easy to play, but will need adult assistance

**Hot tip**

Fisher-Price offers information about child development through play, and parenting advice from experts. In the US, they even offer a newsletter for grandparents.

Another website that children will be keen to visit is Lego's website, at http://www.lego.com/. This site offers a variety of activities to keep children entertained.

1. Choose Play and click Games and then browse the sets of game offered

2. The Action games are designed for older children, with somewhat complicated instructions

3. The Creative section offers several design activities, which may require you to download specific software

4. You can encourage the child to sign in to the free Lego Club. This allows them to save game scores, enter designs into contests and post messages

**Hot tip**

Before introducing children to this website, have a look at some of the games, so that you will be familiar with how they work. You will find it easier to help the child get started.

**Hot tip**

Joining the Lego Club is a way of introducing a child to the concept of an ID and password.

# Basic Skills

When grandchildren come to stay, help them practice their arithmetic, or literacy skills, by playing educational games such as those offered by Knowledge Adventure. This offers a range of math, word, reading, spelling, science and animal games for various ages.

**1** Type www.knowledgeadventure.com and explore the games by age group, subject or category

If you want to help a child begin or improve reading ability, there are websites that specialize in this area. For example:

**1** Go to www.starfall.com, a free public service designed to motivate children to read with phonics

# Homework Help

Yahoo Kids website, at http://kids.yahoo.com, provides reference material suitable for children aged six to twelve.

**Hot tip**

StudyZone separates the educational from the entertainment material, so children can study without distractions.

**1** Click StudyZone tab to focus on academic content

**2** Scroll down to the Directory for links to over 10,000 websites that you can browse or search

**Don't forget**

Human editors review and select everything, and these websites are described as kid-safe and suitable for youngsters to browse.

**3** Click Reference for the Columbia University Press Encyclopedia and American Heritage Dictionary

**4** You can also select the searchable World Factbook

# Learn to Type

**Don't forget**

The Learn 2 Type website is intended for adults, but there are special sections for children and for schools.

Although using the Internet mainly involves the mouse with point and click, being able to use the correct fingering on the keyboard can be a real asset any user, child or adult.

**1** Type kids.learn2type.com into the browser address bar and select the Sign Up button

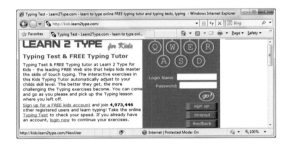

**Don't forget**

There's a typing test and an interactive typing tutor which automatically adjusts to the child's skill level.

**2** For younger children, there's an easy introduction to typing at www.learn2type.com/tots

**Hot tip**

At RapidTyping you can take an online typing test, and download the Typing Tutor for Windows, to practice typing on your computer (no need to be connected).

**3** To improve skill go to www.rapidtyping.com and click RapidTyping then Download RapidTyping

# Art Appreciation

Broaden your grandchild's horizons by introducing them to art through museums and galleries.

**1** The National Gallery of Art has an interactive website for children at www.nga.gov/kids/

**2** Similarly, the Metropolitan Museum of Art offers website www.metmuseum.org/explore/museumkids

**3** If you can't visit in person, go to www.meetmeatthecorner.org/episodes and select Museum Curator at the Metropolitan Museum of Art

**Hot tip**

Faces & Places for example encourages children to create paintings in the style of American native artists, by combining visual elements from more than 100 works from the Gallery's permanent collection.

**Hot tip**

The Timeline is a chronological, geographical, and thematic exploration of the history of art from around the world, as illustrated by the Museum's collection.

**Hot tip**

This is a video that gives a virtual field trip to the museum, to learn about the work of a curator.

# Foreign Languages

If you would like to help the grandchildren practice a foreign language, or want to brush up your vocabulary or grammar, there are many websites that provide free lessons.

**1** Click Languages at www.apples4theteacher.com, for interactive games in Spanish, Polish and Gaelic

## Don't forget

This site also offers practice in American Sign Language, and you can print a set of ASL flash cards.

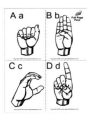

**2** You'll find interactive courses in six different languages at www.busuu.com

## Hot tip

Select Free Online Languages courses and click Take Me To.

You'll also find links to dictionaries, translation services and other resources at this site.

**3** There are links to free courses for about 120 different languages at www.word2word.com, the language resources website

# Science

Science websites for children are plentiful and excellent, and a good place to start is the NASA site www.nasa.gov. This is, as would be expected, a wonderful resource on space, the solar system and exploration.

Don't forget

The NASA Kids Club offers games graded by skill level. Access the site from the Student's page.

**1** From the home page, select For Students. Choose a suitable grade/age for information and games

There are many science museum websites throughout the world, for example the South Kensington Science Museum website, found at www.sciencemuseum.org.uk/.

Hot tip

Subjects range from Art to Transport and the articles vary in approach and length but are easy to read, well illustrated and suitable for most ages.

**2** Select Online Stuff, and explore by subjects, museum objects, news items or through games

# Understand and Play Music

Children can have great fun learning about music with the San Francisco Symphony.

**1** Type the website www.sfskids.org/ into the address bar

**2** Click Skip to bypass the Intro music

**3** Choose the option Instruments of the Orchestra

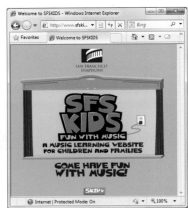

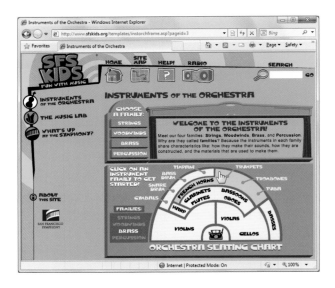

**4** Select a family of instruments to view and listen to the sound of each individual instrument

**5** Alternatively, select the Music Lab, where you learn about tempo, rhythm, pitch and harmony

**6** Choose Instrumentation, where you select different instruments and hear how they affect a composition

# Explore the World

The National Geographic website provides authoritative information at www.nationalgeographic.com/.

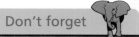
**1** Click the Education tab, and scroll down to find resources specifically for students

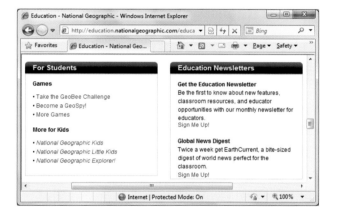

**2** You can introduce them to one of the National Geographic for Kids appropriate to their age

# Help With Revision

There are many websites to help the grandchildren with their revision. The older child can use search engines such as Google, but here are some specific sites to get them started.

**Don't forget**

You should make sure that safe search features are turned on in the search engines. See page 149.

1    Go to www.highschoolace.com for lists of free educational resources, arranged in categories

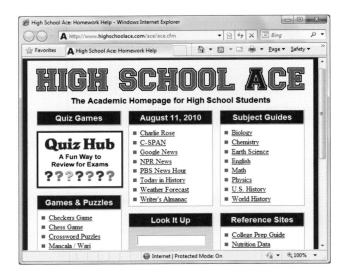

**Hot tip**

You'll find details of colleges, entrance exams and admission criteria in the College Prep Guide.

2    Yahoo has preselected many appropriate references at dir.yahoo.com/education/k_12

**Don't forget**

There are over 30 categories in Yahoo's K-12 (kindergarten through 12th grade) directory.

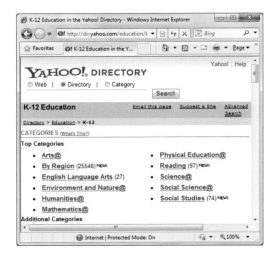

# 11 Keep in Touch

*Whether you are at home or on holiday, the Internet helps you to keep in touch with your family and friends. You can send and receive email, exchange instant messages, or send electronic greetings. With a webcam and software, such as Skype, you can even see one another online.*

# Email Communication

The Internet allows you to communicate with friends, family and business contacts quickly and easily, whether they are just down the street or on the other side of the world. You can send to individuals, or whole groups of people, such as club members, with a simple click of the mouse button. You can include photographs with your email, and attach all kinds of documents, such as Minutes, Agendas and Reports.

Email requires two things – software that allows you to create, save, send and receive messages, and an Internet connection.

**Don't forget**

If you have a dial-up connection, you may prefer to use Outlook or Windows Live Mail at home, as they allow you to compose and read your messages off-line, without paying for connection time.

### Email Software

Microsoft's Outlook and Windows Live Mail can both be used for email. They are programs that are associated with Microsoft Office and Windows, respectively. Outlook is a full Personal Information Manager, which includes an email program. Windows Live Mail has a subset of Outlook functions.

However, many Internet Service Providers offer their own email facility. They allow you to create, send, receive, read and store your email on their server, using your browser. This is known as Webmail, or sometimes Netmail. Its big advantage is that you can access your mail from anywhere in the world – from a friend's PC, a hotel or Internet cafe. It does, however, mean that you must be online when using it.

### Web-based email

Each individual ISP offers their own mailbox structure, but they are all very similar in approach. If you are accustomed to using Outlook or Windows Live Mail, the transition to a web-based facility is very straightforward.

**Hot tip**

When setting up your email account, check to see if your ISP allows Webmail, especially if you anticipate travelling and want to be able to keep in touch.

Some email accounts are normally web-based only, for example Gmail, Hotmail and Yahoo mail. For the purposes of this book, we will be using Yahoo mail.

# Create a Webmail Account

Your ISP may already provide you with a webmail account. However, if you need a new account, you can create one at Yahoo.com:

**1** Go to website www.yahoo.com, move the mouse pointer over Yahoo! Mail, then click Sign up

**2** Enter your details. As you type, Yahoo explains how it uses the particular piece of information

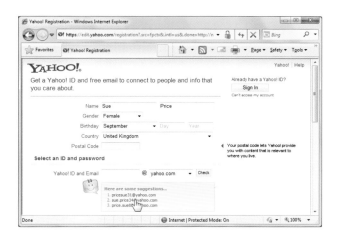

**3** Select one of the suggested IDs, or type in your preferred ID, complete the requested details, then click Create My Account

**Don't forget**

If you already have a Yahoo ID, you can click Sign in and enter your ID and password.

**Don't forget**

The verification process is used to prevent automated registrations. You must be able to read the monitor to type in the letters – something that can only be achieved with the human eye.

# The Webmail Window

With your mail account now set up, go to www.yahoo.com and sign in, then select Yahoo! Mail from My Favorites.

Sign in to Yahoo!
Yahoo! ID:
sue.price34@yahoo.com
(e.g. free2rhyme@yahoo.com)
Password:
••••••••
Sign In

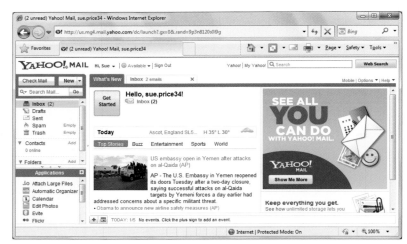

The Yahoo mail screen opens on the What's New tab, which provides current news items. The second tab shows the currently selected email folder, initially the Inbox, and the number of email messages it contains.

The Folders panel, on the left of the page, displays your current folders and allows you to organize your mail.

- the Inbox is where your mail arrives. To view your new mail, click on the Inbox folder, or the Inbox tab

- Drafts is where you will store any incomplete messages, or ones that you do not want to send immediately

- the Sent folder keeps a copy of email sent

- the Spam folder will contain any messages that the Yahoo spamguard program isolates as unwanted

- Trash contains any messages that are no longer required

- Contacts gives you access to your Contact list

- Below the folders there is the Applications list

**Beware**

The Yahoo mail sign-in screen offers the option to remember your password. This is fine in a domestic situation, but do not select it on anyone else's PC, or in an Internet cafe. See also page 218 (delete browsing history).

☐ **Keep me signed in**
for 2 weeks unless I sign out. Info
[Uncheck if on a shared computer]

**Don't forget**

Spam is the term applied to unwanted, unsolicited and inappropriate messages. Yahoo provides a Spamguard program to scan emails for such messages, and it is automatically switched on when you sign up with a new ID.

# Access Your Mail

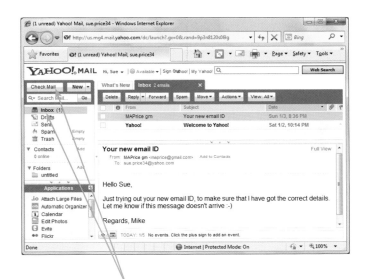

**Hot tip**

Click the checkbox next to each message in the Inbox to select it. You can select multiple messages and then click Delete, Spam, etc.

**Hot tip**

The contents of the selected message are displayed in the preview area below the list of messages.

**1** Click on Check Mail, or the Inbox folder in the left panel, to show new messages. The number of unread messages is shown, e.g. (1)

**2** Select a message and double-click the subject (or click Full View) to open the message on a new tab

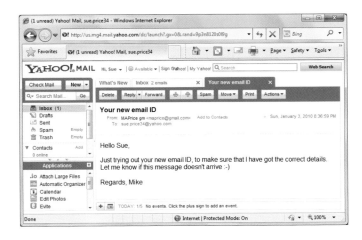

**Don't forget**

Messages remain in the Inbox until you Delete, mark as Spam, or Move them to a different folder.

**3** Select from the options to Delete, Reply, Forward, mark as Spam or Move to another folder, or choose the Previous or Next buttons

# Create and Send Mail

**1** Click New on the Mail window to create a new message (or click the down arrow to select Chat or Text message). The New Email Message window opens on a new tab

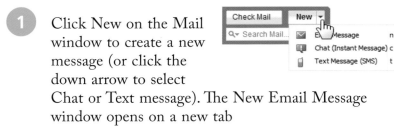

**2** Select the recipient, either by typing their address, or by clicking on the To: button, to add addresses from your Contacts

**3** Press the Tab key, or click in the Subject box, and type in the topic of the email

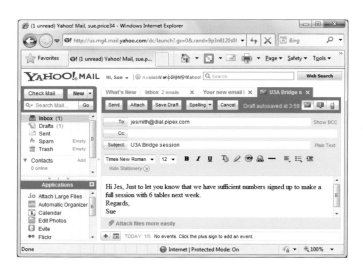

**4** Tab again to the message area, which offers standard word processing tools, such as font styles and spell checking. Type your message and click Send

**5** You get confirmation that the message has been sent. Click OK and the message tab closes and you return to the previous tab

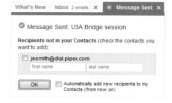

# Manage Your Mail

Webmail ISPs allocate you storage space on their server when you sign up for their email facility. Yahoo, for example, now gives you unlimited storage, as long as you abide by normal email rules and do not abuse the system.

## Sort your messages

**1** Click in the header area on Sender or Subject to sort alphabetically, click again to sort in reverse order

**2** Click Date to sort your messages newest to oldest or again to sort in reverse order

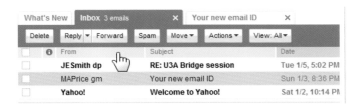

## Manage your messages

**1** Click in the box to the left of the message to select it (insert a tick). Click again to remove the tick. You can tick as many messages at a time as you wish. The messages can then be managed as one

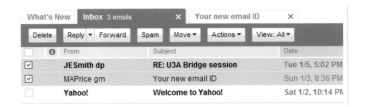

## Delete your messages

**1** Click Delete to transfer all selected messages to the Trash folder. Messages in the Trash folder do not count towards your total storage

**171**

**Hot tip**

Sort your messages, newest to oldest, to have your new email appear at the top of the Inbox.

**Hot tip**

Tick the box next to the left of From to select or deselect all messages.

**Don't forget**

Messages will remain in the Trash folder, allowing you to reinstate them if necessary. Click on Empty to empty the Trash folder.

# Create and Use Folders

To create folders for webmail storage:

**1** Click Add, next to My Folders in the side panel, and the new folder will appear in the folder list

**2** Type the folder name and click away from the folder name to create it. The new folder replaces the Inbox tab

**3** Click back on the Inbox in the folder list to open it

**4** The next time you click the Move button, you will have the option to move selected items to the new folder

**5** You can also drag and drop a message into a folder

**6** To rename or delete a folder, right-click the folder and choose the required option. There are also options to empty the Spam or Trash folders

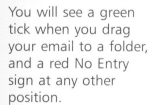

**7** Click the arrow next to Folders to Hide your list of folders

**8** Click the arrow again to Show folders

# Webmail Options

Customize your webmail account and take advantage of features offered by your ISP, using Options on the main Mail window and selecting Mail Options.

## Spam

SpamGuard is on when you sign up to Yahoo. Click on Spam to change settings, such as how long to keep spam messages and where to move allowed messages.

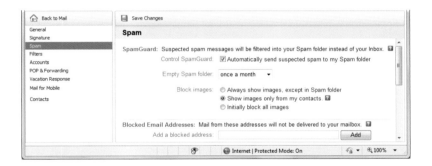

## Blocked Addresses

This allows you to block messages from your Inbox for up to 500 addresses or domain names. The blocked messages will be deleted before you see them.

## Filters

Filters are applied to your incoming mail. Use filters to automatically sort your mail into appropriate folders. Click on Filters, then Add and complete the details.

Hot tip

Other webmail options include adding an automatic signature, setting an auto response when you are away or on holiday, and setting your general preferences.

173

Don't forget

Webmail providers will also offer more sophisticated functions, improved filters, larger amounts of storage, etc. on a chargeable basis.

# Attachments

You can attach documents and photos to the messages you send using your webmail account.

**1** Create your email in the usual way and click the Attach button to locate attachments for the message

**Don't forget**

You can attach files up to a total message size of 25Mb.

**Don't forget**

Messages with one or more attached files will have the paperclip symbol appended.

**2** The Documents folder will open. Select the file, or navigate your PC's folders to locate and select the required file. Click Open. Repeat to attach more files

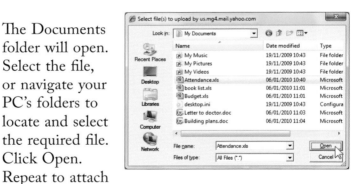

**3** The file(s) will be checked for viruses

**4** Complete your email and then click Send

**5** If you change your mind about a file, click Remove before you send the message

# Receive Attachments

When you receive a file with an attachment:

**1** Check that you know the sender. If you are unsure of the source, then be on your guard

**2** Open the message, the attachment will be indicated in the email header area

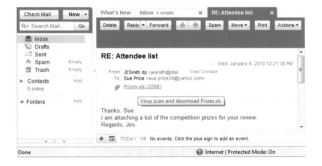

**3** Click the file name. The attachment is immediately scanned for viruses and a status report given

**4** Click Download Attachment. You can then select to Open or Save the attachment. Normally you would select Save and then choose the appropriate folder if necessary

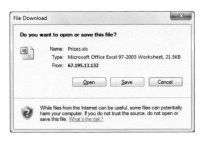

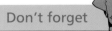

**Beware**

You should always scan attachments for viruses, even if you know the sender. Yahoo webmail provides a virus scanner. Check your provider to see what it offers.

**Don't forget**

You may need to select a new destination folder, as the computer will remember the previous destination of a downloaded file, and will open that folder automatically.

175

# eCards

You can send all kinds of free greeting cards to friends and family using the Internet. Search for a website, for example:

**1** Go to www.google.com and search for free ecards online

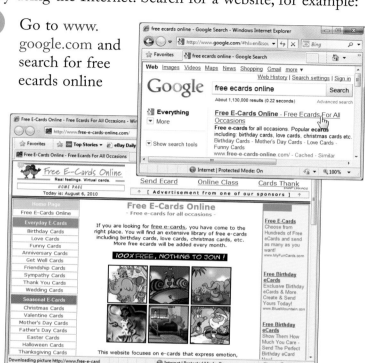

**2** Choose a category, select a card from those shown and provide the email and message details desired

## E-postcards

Check the website for your holiday destination to see if free digital postcards are offered. For example:

**1** Go to the website at www.westvirginianetwork.com, and select the option to Send an ePostcard

# Instant Messaging

Many ISPs and other software companies provide Instant Messaging services. This service allows you to communicate with a selected list of contacts, either by typing your message or by voice. With a camera attached to your PC, you can even transmit (and receive) video.

For this, you will need to download and install special software. In this example we shall use Skype, which is available at no charge and provides full video service.

**1** Visit www.skype.com and click the Download tab, and then click the Download Now button

**2** Internet Explorer may ask you to confirm the download

**3** Save the file to disk, then run the setup program to install the Skype software

**Don't forget**

You will need a full ADSL (broadband) service to use Instant Messaging with video.

177

**Hot tip**

Just follow the on-screen prompts and accept the defaults suggested.

SkypeSetup.exe
Skype
Skype Technologies S.A.

# Sign Up to Skype

When you start Skype for the first time you will need to sign in and create an identity for yourself.

**1** Supply your name, Skype name and password. As with the Yahoo ID, you may need to try several Skype names to find one that's available

### Don't forget

You will be offered the option to Sign me in when Skype starts. Clear the box if you'd prefer not to sign in automatically.

**2** Then follow the on-screen instructions, supplying an email address and your location, if you wish

**3** When you sign in, you'll see the Skype Welcome Screen. This provides a brief tutorial and also allows you to check your audio and video configuration

### Hot tip

Similarly, you can clear the box labelled Show the Welcome Screen at startup, and it will be hidden in future.

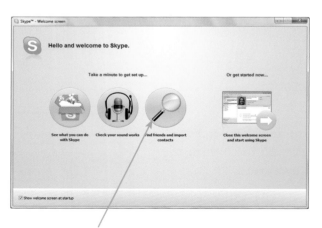

You can also find friends, and import address book entries, to add them to your Skype contacts (see page 179).

# Add Contacts

**1** On the Welcome Screen, click the option to Find friends and import contacts

**Hot tip**

If Skype cannot locate a person from your contacts list, search the Skype directory.

**Hot tip**

For Outlook, you must select Contact, Show Outlook contacts. Some email services are not supported, for example Outlook Express.

**179**

**2** Select the email service you use (e.g. Gmail), type the user name and password and select Import

Skype scans your address book and lists entries that it recognizes as having Skype accounts. Select those that you want to add to your Skype contacts list.

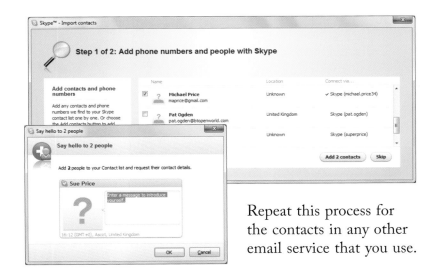

**Don't forget**

Your contacts must confirm their wish to join your list, and vice-versa when they ask you to join.

Repeat this process for the contacts in any other email service that you use.

# Make a Call

## Don't forget

If your contact has supplied a landline or mobile phone number, and you click on that, Skype will presume that you wish to call that number, rather than connect via the Internet. You will need to purchase credit from Skype to use those methods.

**1** Your first call should be to check your installation, so select the Echo / Sound Test Service entry in your contacts list and click the Call button. A voice will ask you to record a ten second message, which will be played back to you if your system is working correctly

**2** To connect with a friend, select their name and click on the Call (green phone) or the Video Call button

**3** You will hear a ringing tone. If your friend is online they will be informed that you are calling. If they are off-line, you will be informed

## Hot tip

Your contacts will be able to see if you are online. To change your status, click the small tick on the Status bar and select a different option, especially if you don't wish to be interrupted.

**4** If the call is accepted, you can type instant messages, have a live conversation (using your microphone) or have a video session (using your web camera)

**5** Click the Video button to turn video display on or off

**6** Click the End Call (red phone) button to terminate the conversation

# 12 Publish to the Internet

*Become completely involved in the Internet phenomenon by creating your own website, and let other web users visit your web pages. If you represent a non-profit or volunteer group, you can set up a website on their behalf. You can also access feeds to stay up to the minute with changes on interesting websites.*

# Build a Website

If you have something to share, why not create your own pages on the web? Think of things you might want to publish in your website. It doesn't have to be for business. It could be just for fun, so you can learn first hand about the way the Internet operates. It might be a place where you store information related to a hobby, or interest, that you'd like to share with others who have the same interests. You might have project reports, how-to guides, book reports, photographs or links to associated web pages.

Whatever you want to put in your website, you will need three main items:

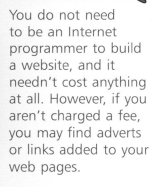

**1** Storage space on the Internet to record the text and images that you want to share

**2** Tools and facilities to help you assemble and arrange those components into the form of a website

**3** An Internet address that you can give to others so that they can view your website

Your Internet Service Provider may make web space available, as part of your Internet account, and provide the addressing needed. They would also provide or recommend suitable tools and techniques for building and publishing your web page. However, often the ISP facilities are limited to a predefined home page that may limit what you are able to achieve. Creating your website at the ISP would also make it harder for you to switch suppliers, if your requirements were to change.

Fortunately, there are many other Internet services that will meet all of the requirements for building web pages. For some, it is their main business and they will require a monthly or annual fee, except, perhaps, for the initial trial period. Others, such as Google, may already be providing other services and will offer web page creation as an additional free feature.

# Find Free Website Services

Website services offering free building and hosting change nature over time. For example, Geocities.com was founded in 1995, and was taken over in 1999 by Yahoo, but continued to offer free website services. However, in 2009, it was replaced by the fee-based Yahoo Web Hosting service.

To see the range of services currently offered:

**1** Go to Google and search for free websites

**2** You'll get millions of matching web pages, and lots of advertisements – free doesn't necessarily mean there's no profit potential, as you'll soon discover

**3** Review the services that are listed, to see how they meet your needs, investigating issues such as:
- The type of website allowed (personal or business)
- Advertising policy (banners, pop-ups, frames)
- Amount of web space provided
- File and web page upload restrictions
- Use of programming languages, e.g. PHP and Perl
- Traffic limitations that may be imposed

**Don't forget**

While a free website may be ideal for gaining experience, always remember that the service could be withdrawn without notice. Keep backups of your material and have a fall-back plan just in case.

183

**Hot tip**

You should really experiment with a service before making a commitment, since some constraints may not be obvious until you start working with the system.

# Webs (Freewebs)

Webs started out in 2001 as Freewebs, but changed its name in 2008. It provides many facilities for websites, including blogs, forums, calendars, guestbooks, webstores and photo galleries. The basic service is free but there are paid premium services, such as removal of on-site advertisements and the inclusion of more advanced features. To get started:

**1** Go to the website www.webs.com

**2** Enter your email address and a password then click Create a Website

## Create Your WebsID

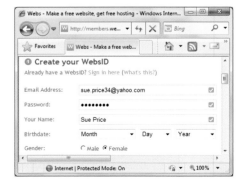

**1** Enter your name as you wish it to appear in the website profile

**2** Enter your birth date and gender

## Set Up Your Site

**1** Provide the site address (the subdomain name)

**2** Add the site title

**3** Select the site type (personal, organization, or business) and the site category

## Select a Template for Your Site

**1** Choose a template and color or alignment option

**2** Accept terms of service and Continue to the next step

### Don't forget

You continue to be prompted, and you are given warnings, or confirmation, as you enter the data.

### Hot tip

There are different categories suggested for each of the website types (see page 198), but the 300 templates are available for all the categories.

185

# Customize Your Site

## Make Revisions

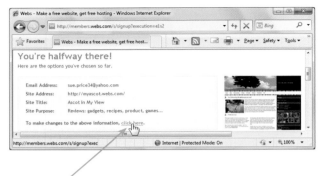

**1**  Click here, as indicated, to make any revisions needed

## Choose Pages for Your Site

Suitable pages are preselected for the type and category of website that you have chosen, and some options are offered.

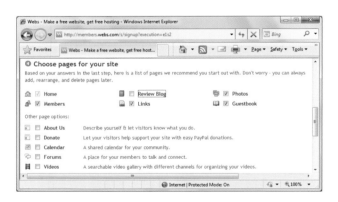

**1**  You can add or remove any of the pages, except for the Home page, which is always required

**2**  Select the button to Create my Site

# Create the Website

**1** Select the Webs package you want - Basic, Enhanced or Pro, or click No Thanks, Continue for a free site

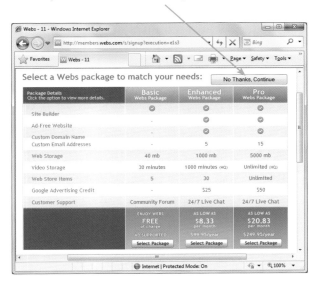

## Hot tip

Webs.com gives you the reasons why you might choose to upgrade, but makes the free account available forever! Your site will remain live, for free, as long as you continue to log in to your Webs account. They recommend logging in at least once a month.

**2** The Webs SiteBuilder (a WYSIWYG editor) is loaded

**3** Webs SiteBuilder is now ready to update your website files. Click the Content Box button to add information to the Home page

## Don't forget

Click the X button to save the draft website and return to the Site Manager, where you can Log out and make your changes later.

# Edit the Website

**1** Open www.webs.com and sign in using the email address and password you specified for your account

## Hot tip

If your websites aren't listed, click the link to Attach them here. They'll be added to the list of sites you've created.

**2** Click Edit This Site for the new website you created

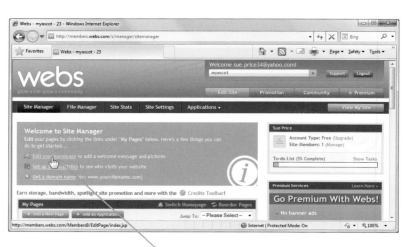

## Don't forget

You can also sign in, using the website address and password, and go straight to the Site Manager.

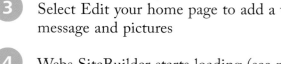

**3** Select Edit your home page to add a welcome message and pictures

**4** Webs SiteBuilder starts loading (see page 187)

# ...cont'd

**5** When the Webs SiteBuilder has loaded and opened the Home page, click Content Box (see page 187)

**6** Click in the first box and type the title, then click in the second box and type, or paste, the text content

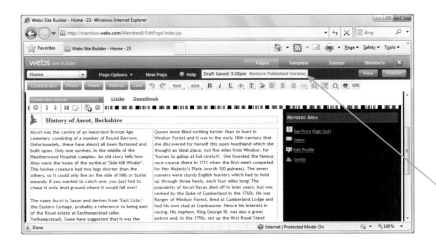

**7** When you click in a box, the Content Box Options bar is displayed, with functions, such as resequence boxes, split a box into columns, add a new box and delete the selected box

**Hot tip**

Use this page editor to add title, text, photos, videos and addons. It works just like a word processor, with a format bar that allows you to change font style, size and colors, edit and undo edits, align text, and add items using drag-n-drop, etc.

**Don't forget**

The editor saves all changes in a draft version of the page, but you can revert to the published version at any time, to cancel the recent changes.

# Insert an Image

**1** In Webs SiteBuilder, click in the box, then select the Photo button to insert an image

**2** The first time you do this, you may be told that you haven't uploaded any images yet, so click Upload

For subsequent inserts, your uploaded images will be displayed, or you can click Upload New Image to get another image.

**3** Select Browse, then locate and open the image file

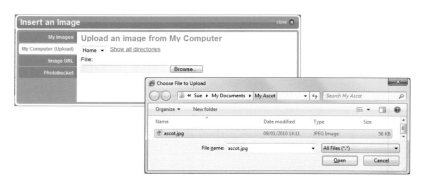

Hot tip

You can upload images ahead of time, using the File Manager (see page 193).

**4** The image is inserted at the selected point in the box

# View the Web Page

When you have made changes to your home page, you can view the results in your browser.

**1** In the Webs SiteBuilder, click the View button to view this page

**2** You'll be warned if there are changes to the page that have not yet been published

**3** Click Publish Page to view the latest version, and the page will be published with the changes

**4** Select View again, and the web page will now be shown in a browser window

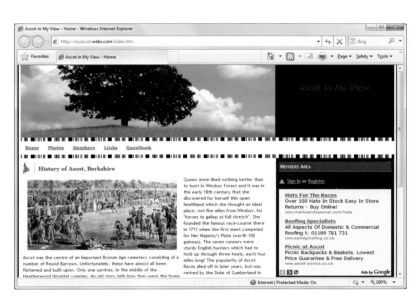

**5** Close the web page, then select the X button (see page 187) to close Webs SiteBuilder and return to the Site Manager, from where you can also view the website

---

**Hot tip**

You would select Continue without publishing, to view the previous version of the page.

**Don't forget**

The web page is addressed by the subdomain name, e.g. myascot.webs.com. The index.htm is the name of the home page. Note that some adverts, appropriate to the page contents, have been added.

# Site Manager

The Site Manager is where you can add, edit and remove pages from your website. These can be regular pages, like the example Home page, where you add free-form content using SiteBuilder, or structured pages, such as Photo or Video Galleries, Guestbooks and Forums.

**Hot tip**

Beside Site Manager you'll find the File Manager, Site Stats, Site Settings and Applications buttons.

**Hot tip**

When you have responded to the email, Webs.com updates the status of your to-do list.

1  Click a page to edit it using SiteBuilder (see page 195 for a Photo Gallery example)

2  Click Show Tasks to see the progress to date, in building your website

3  Select a task, for example Verify your Email

4  Check your email for a Welcome to Webs.com message and click the link provided

# File Manager

**1** Click the File Manager button to list your files

**Hot tip**

The File Manager provides ways to upload the files you need, shows a list of what's uploaded, and allows you to edit, rename, or delete selected files.

**Don't forget**

If you choose Optimize Pictures and Videos for the web, images larger than 800x600 are reduced, and video files are converted to swf, or Flash files, to reduce the space needed and improve display speed.

**2** Select Single File Uploader to load one file at a time (as with the SiteBuilder upload)

**3** Multiple File Uploader is for Premium users only, so try Super Multi Uploader to transfer several files at once. However, it may not work on all systems

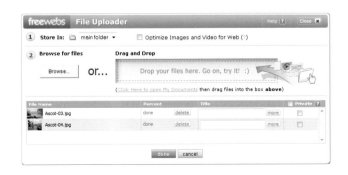

# Upload Files via Email

You can email image files as attachments, straight to your Webs account, as long as you have verified the email address for your account (see page 192).

(see page 192)

### Hot tip

Currently, only media files are allowed, i.e. image files (.jpg, .gif, .png), audio files (.wav, .mp3, .midi, .mpeg), video files (.mov, .avi, .wmv), and flash files (.swf).

**1** Send an email with media file attachments to save@ webs.com

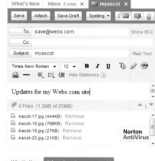

**2** The attached files will automatically upload to your Webs account

**3** You'll get confirmation that the files have been received and stored in your account

**4** The files you uploaded to your account will appear in File Manager, in a folder called Emailed

### Beware

If you have more than one Webs account, you must put the user name of the target account in the Subject line of the email.

### Don't forget

You can upload up to 10Mb of files at one time, subject to the storage limit on your account.

**5** To Move the files, click the Action box and select the main folder [myascot], or any other folder you may have created

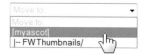

# Photo Gallery

To set up the photo gallery on your website:

**1** From Site Manager, click to edit the Photos page

Hot tip

If your website doesn't have a Photos page, select the Add an Application button, then choose the Photo Gallery application.

**2** From SiteBuilder, select Add Photos, then upload pictures, or select from pictures you've already uploaded

**3** Click Submit to create your photo album, then add titles, captions and adjust the sequence of photos

Don't forget

You can choose a photo as the album cover. Scroll down to select Save when you've finished.

## ...cont'd

**4** Use drag and drop to resequence the photos

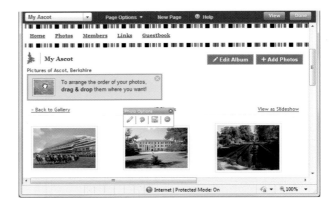

**5** Select View to open the website at the Photos page, with the contents of the album displayed

**6** Select Photos from the navigation bar to see the album view

**7** Close the website and select Done to complete the creation and update of your photo album

# Complete Site Information

**1** From Site Manager, select Show Tasks and select the task Complete Site Information

**2** You are reminded that effective descriptions can help the visibility of websites on the Internet

### Hot tip

You can also click the Site Settings button to complete or amend the site information.

**Site Settings**

**3** Select the Edit Site Information button and fill in the details that will best describe your website

I can help you get more visibility for your site, but you first need to fill out your site's description, category, and keywords. This will help tell search engines like Google know more about your site. Do it and you will also get listed higher in the Webs Directory!

**Edit Site Information**

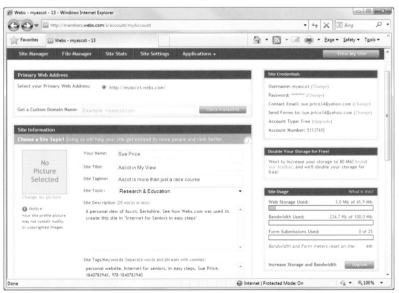

### Beware

Put 25 words or less in the description box, or the changes will be rejected.

**4** Add your site to the Webs Directory, then click the Save Changes button

☑ Include site in the Webs Directory
**Save Changes**

**5** The information is saved and you can continue building your site

Your Site Information has been saved.
Close this notice

### Don't forget

Select the Support button to open the Webs Support Portal, where you'll find lots of help and access to user forums.

**Support**

# Charity Websites

When you set up your site with Webs.com (see page 184-5), you could select Groups/Orgs and Associations, or Small Business/Prof and Non-Profit Organization.

If it is a registered charity or other qualifying organization, you may be to able to take advantage of specialist support.

1   See www. pro-webdesign.biz/free-website-for-charity. html for information on free web design for charities

2   For assistance with website design, you could also go to www.charityfocus.org and click the Nonprofit tab

# RSS Web Feeds

The Feeds icon on the Internet Explorer toolbar tells you if Web feeds are available, summaries of website changes, e.g. headlines on CNN, or new posts in blogs. On some websites this is greyed (inactive). Hover over it and you are told No feeds detected. On other sites, the icon changes color and becomes active, and you can View feeds. A Green icon means there are Web slices also

**Hot tip**

RSS stands for Really Simple Syndication, and is used to describe the technology used in creating feeds. A Web feed is a summary of website changes, e.g. headlines on CNN, or new posts in blogs. A Web Slice is a specific portion of a web page that you can subscribe to, and get updates.

1    At www.nytimes.com, click the arrow next to the Feeds icon, to see the list of available feeds

2    At www.cnn.com, you'll also see Web slices

3    Click an entry to view the feed at its website. Click Subscribe to this feed, to ask for regular updates

4    Click the Subscribe button to add this to your Feeds list in your Favorites Center

5    You have now subscribed for updates of the chosen feed

**Hot tip**

The Feeds feature is managed in the same way as your Favorites, so you can organize entries into subfolders, storing related feeds together under the same heading (see page 27).

# View Feeds

**1** To view your subscribed feeds, click the Favorites button, and then click the Feeds tab

**2** Select a feed from the list to see the latest entries for that particular feed

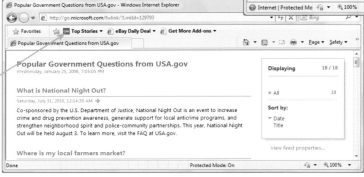

**3** Click the Favorites button as above, then click the arrow icon at the top to fix the Feeds list

**4** Now you can select and review the individual feeds, without having to reselect Favorites for each in turn. Click the [X] button to hide the list again

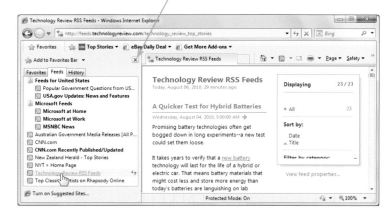

# 13 Social Networking

*Online communities, in the form of blogs and social networks, have become even more popular than email, with online users. Find out what they are, how to participate, and how they can give you, or a friend, a reason to keep on going.*

# Online Communities

The Internet has created a whole new way of grouping people according to interests, experiences, or activities, in the form of the social networking website.

This type of website creates an online community of Internet users. When you join, you can read the profile pages of other members to get to know about them and you can contact them by instant messaging, telephone or video. You may find the membership is very diverse, being open to individuals from all around the world. You can, however, create your own network of friends within that online community, by locating those who share common interests or goals.

Do proceed with caution when getting to know people online, just as you would when meeting strangers at clubs and bars. By being aware of the potential risks, and using common sense, you should be able to safely participate in and enjoy social networking.

There are hundreds of social networking websites. We discuss a few of the more familiar ones in the next few pages, but you can find a more comprehensive list of active social networking sites at en.wikipedia.org/wiki/List_of_social_networking_websites.

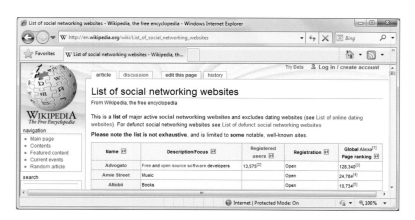

## Don't forget

You are already part of several social networks, the neighborhood, the work place, or your club, for example.

## Beware

There are dangers associated with social networking, including data theft and viruses. The most prevalent danger though, often involves individuals who claim to be someone they are not.

## Hot tip

This has almost 200 websites, with a brief description and focus, number of members, type of registration and global ranking. Click the name for a detailed review.

# Blogs

People have always kept a daily journal. Samuel Pepys started his in 1659, and is famed for it to this day. Captain Cook kept a journal, as did many politicians. Even the fictional Adrian Mole and Bridget Jones kept diaries.

Today, everyone can do it, with the aid of the Internet and a web log, usually shortened to blog. This is a website where the entries are dated (and regularly updated) and displayed in reverse order, latest at the top. They have feedback systems to allow readers to add their comments.

Style and taste in blogs vary enormously. To get a flavour of the range, view a variety of blogs.

**1** Go to blogsearch.google.com and search on a topic

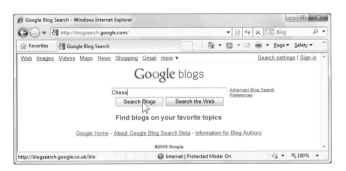

You will get a list of related blogs, if there are entire blogs dedicated to your topic, plus a selection of individual blog posts that are associated with your topic.

## Hot tip

Blogs are perhaps the simplest form of social networking, often related to a particular topic, such as food, politics, or local news.

## Beware

Blogsearch may start with a predefined search of news stories, automatically chosen and sequenced, but you can ignore these and enter your own search keywords.

## Don't forget

The news media and the business world have caught on to blogging, so you will encounter blogs that are commercial in content and purpose. Just skip on to the next in line.

# Create a Blog

If you'd like to try blogging, go to www.blogspot.com and click the link Create a Blog.

**1** Select Sign in First to your existing Google account

**2** Specify the email address and password for your Google account and click Sign in

**3** If asked, type the verification word or phrase, to confirm you are an actual user

# Post to Your Blog

**1** Provide the blog title and the blog address (URL), then click Continue

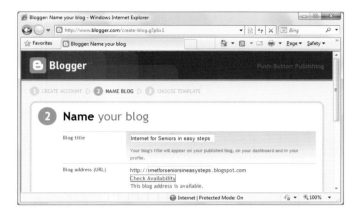

### Don't forget

The blog address is part of a web address for your blog, so it should be lower case letters, numbers and hyphens only. Check Availability tells you if the name is in use.

**2** Choose a template and click Continue

### Hot tip

You can change or replace the template after your blog has been created, and add features to it.

**3** Your blog will be created. Click Start Blogging to post your first message

### Don't forget

You provide the title and text for your post (blog entry), then click Publish Post to make it visible at the blog site.

# Facebook

Facebook started in 2004 and now has more than 350 million active users worldwide. It is open to anyone aged 13 and over. You add friends, and send messages and update your personal profile to tell them what's happening with you. When you add friends they must add you as a friend as well.

**1** To join, go to www.facebook.com, provide name, email, password, gender and DoB, then click Sign Up

**Don't forget**

Your real date of birth is required to encourage authenticity, but you can hide this from your profile if you wish.

**2** Enter the two words provided as a Security check. Then click Sign Up to accept the terms of use and the privacy policy

**Hot tip**

If you just want to browse Facebook to start with, you can delay entering your full details until you are more comfortable with the website.

**3** Let Facebook search your email address book to locate friends who already have accounts (or select Skip this step, to leave the search until later)

# Create a Facebook Account

**1** Fill in your profile details (school, university and company) to help locate friends (or Skip for now)

**2** Upload a photo of yourself from the computer, or take a photo with your webcam (or skip for now)

**Don't forget**

If you want your friends to be able to find you on Facebook, put as much detail as you feel able to share. In particular, put a real photo of yourself, so your friends know it really is you.

**3** Check your email to confirm your Facebook account

**Hot tip**

Click on the link in the Facebook Confirmation message to complete your registration.

# Facebook Privacy Policy

**Hot tip**

When you log in, you see the options to find people and update details that you may have skipped. However, firstly check the privacy policy.

**1** When you log in after confirming your email, select Control what information you share

**2** The guide to privacy on Facebook is displayed

**Hot tip**

Whichever social networking service you decide to join, make sure it offers a suitable privacy policy, so you can protect the information that's important to you.

Information and posts that make it easier for friends to find, identify, and learn about you should be available to Everyone.

The more personal information and details, such as religious and political views, should be restricted to Friends of Friends.

Your contact information, such as mobile phone number and email address, should only be visible to Friends.

**Don't forget**

When you view and edit your profile, you can choose whether details, such as gender and birth date or age, are shown.

Until their eighteenth birthday, minors who use Facebook have their information restricted to Friends of Friends. (See page 147-151 for more on protecting children).

# Twitter

Twitter started in 2006 and now has 44 million members. Its users send and read messages known as tweets. These are text-based posts of up to 140 characters, displayed on the author's profile page and delivered to the author's subscribers, who are known as followers.

Senders can restrict delivery to those in their circle of friends or, by default, allow open access. Users can send and receive tweets via the Twitter website, Short Message Service (SMS), or external applications.

**1** Go to www.twitter.com and click Sign up now

**2** Follow the prompts to provide your name, user name, password, email address and confirming text

**3** Twitter will offer to search for your friends using your address book, but you can skip this

**4** Twitter also offers a list of Twitter users that you might wish to follow. Again, you can skip this

**5** A confirmation email will be sent, and you must access this to complete the registration

> **Please confirm your account — a confirmation message was sent to sue.price34@yahoo.com**
> Until you confirm, you will have limited access to certain features on Twitter. Learn more
> Resend confirmation - Change email address

**Don't forget**

This process is similar to Facebook, except that Twitter needs a user name which becomes part of the URL, used to access your account, e.g. twitter.com/sueprice34

> **sueprice34**
>
> Your URL: http://twitter.com/**sueprice34**

# Find Someone to Follow

1. Sign in using your user name (or email address) and your password

2. Click Find People and type the name of someone you want to follow

3. Select one of the results and check the details (in this case there's only one Hayley Westenra)

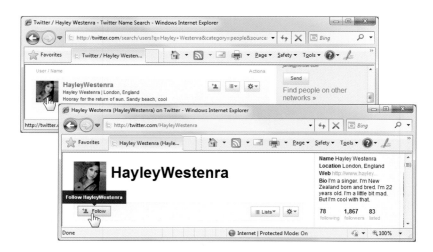

4. Select Follow to add the person to your list, so you'll see all the updates they make

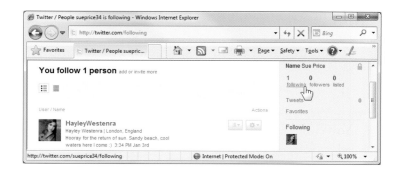

# YouTube

YouTube is a video sharing website on which users can upload and share videos. It uses Adobe Flash Video to display a wide variety of user-generated video content, including movie clips, TV clips, and music videos, as well as amateur content, such as video blogging and short original videos. Most of the content on YouTube has been uploaded by individuals, although media corporations, including CBS and the BBC, offer some of their material.

1    To view the videos, go to www.youtube.com

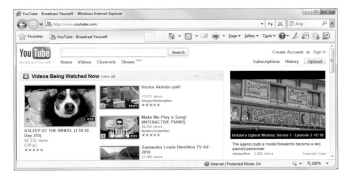

2    There's no need to register or enter personal details, just type the name and keywords into the Search box

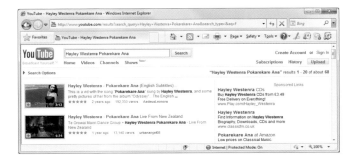

3    The results are displayed, in this case a total of 68

4    YouTube also takes the opportunity to display adverts related to your search topic

**Don't forget**

Videos that contain potentially offensive content are available only to registered users over the age of 18. The terms of service prohibit uploading videos containing questionable material.

**Hot tip**

Unregistered users can watch the videos, while registered users are permitted to upload an unlimited number of videos.

**Don't forget**

Viewing YouTube videos requires the Adobe Flash player to be installed on your computer. Video formats from 320x240 to 1920x1080 are supported.

# A Reason to Keep on Going

**1** Go to www.nytimes.com and type in the search box a reason to keep on going, then click Search

**2** Select the June 2, 2009 article by Stephanie Clifford

# 14 Internet Security

*You need to take care when you visit the Internet, since it has become a target for identity theft. However, there are many ways in which you can protect yourself from risk.*

# Browser Security

Internet Explorer 8 incorporates a series of enhancements to help protect your system from attackers. These include:

### Automatic Tab Crash Recovery
If a website or add-on causes a tab to hang in IE8, that tab is recovered. The browser itself and other tabs are unaffected

### SmartScreen Filter
This helps protect you from phishing attacks, online fraud, spoofed websites and malicious software

### Add-on Manager
This lets you disable or allow web browser add-ons and delete unwanted ActiveX controls

### Pop-up Blocker
You can limit, or block, most pop-ups, choosing the level of blocking you prefer

### Delete Browsing History
Clear the information stored on your computer when you visit various websites

### InPrivate Browsing and Filtering
This allows you to surf the web without leaving a trail that can be seen, or exploited, by websites or by other users

### Domain Name Highlighting
The domain name in the address bar is highlighted to help you confirm you are visiting a legitimate website

### Cross-Site Scripting Filter
The CSS filter provides higher security levels to help protect you from hackers and web attacks

### Windows Defender
IE8 integrates with Windows Defender to provide live scanning of Web downloads to protect against spyware

### Parental Controls and Family Safety
IE8 works with these to provide safer browsing for children

# SmartScreen Filter

This is turned on by default, and operates in the background. If it finds suspicious web pages, it displays messages. It also checks sites you visit against a dynamic list of reported phishing sites. If it finds a match, you get a warning screen:

**1**  Type 207.68.169.170/contoso/enroll_auth.html (a special test website) and press Enter

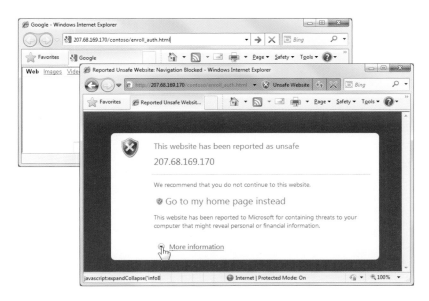

Hot tip

Online phishing is a way to trick users into revealing information. It starts with an email that appears to be from a trusted source. Recipients are directed to a fake website, which asks for data, which is then misused.

**215**

Beware

Be very sure of the website, before continuing against the advice from the SmartScreen filter.

**2**  The website has been reported as unsafe, so you are recommended not to continue

**3**  Click More Information for details or to over-ride

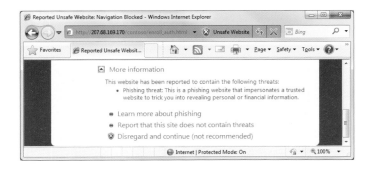

Don't forget

SmartScreen Filter also checks files downloaded from the web and, again, warns you if it finds a match.

# Add-on Manager

If you believe that a new add-on is causing problems on your system, for example generating irritating messages or causing Internet Explorer problems, you can disable it.

**1** Click Tools, Manage Add-ons to view a list of the add-ons installed on your system, (sorted by publisher)

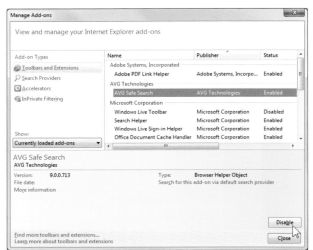

**2** Select the add-on, click Disable, click Close, then restart Internet Explorer

**3** Switching off AVG Safe Search will prevent AVG from checking search results and displaying validations

# Pop-up Blocking

The Pop-up Blocker is turned on in Internet Explorer by default and will block most pop-ups. To try this out:

**1** Visit the website www.popuptest.com, then scroll down and select a test, such as Mouseover PopUp

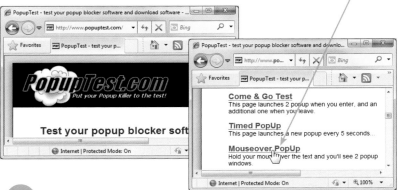

**2** Move the mouse over the text as instructed, and the message Pop-up blocked is displayed on the Information bar at the top

**3** Click the Information bar and choose to temporarily allow pop-ups at this site (for the current visit only)

**4** Choose to always allow pop-ups from this site, to have them appear on future visits

**5** If the Information Bar isn't displayed, click Tools, Pop-up Blocker, to display the list of options and to change pop-up blocker settings

# Delete Browsing History

As you browse the web, Internet Explorer stores details of the websites you visit and data that you type into web forms. The information Internet Explorer stores includes:

- Favorite websites data
- Temporary Internet files
- Cookies
- History of your website visits
- Data entered into web forms
- Saved Passwords
- InPrivate Filtering data

Storing this information is intended to improve your web browsing speed, but you may want to delete the recorded details if you're cleaning up your computer, or if you have been using a public computer.

**1** Click Tools, and then click Delete Browsing History

**2** Select, or clear, the boxes to determine which data you want to preserve or delete

**3** Click Delete, and then close Internet Explorer when deletion completes, to clear cookies from memory

# InPrivate Browsing/Filtering

InPrivate Browsing prevents Internet Explorer from storing data about your browsing session. This helps prevent anyone else, who might be using your computer, from seeing where you visited and what you looked at on the web.

## Hot tip

You can also open a new tab, and on that tab click Open an InPrivate Browsing window.

**1** Select Safety, then click InPrivate Browsing

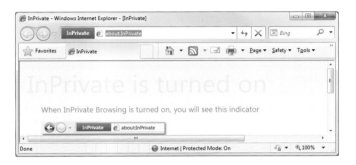

**2** To end InPrivate Browsing, close that window

InPrivate Filtering helps prevent website content providers from collecting information about sites you visit.

**1** Select Safety, then click InPrivate Filtering

## Beware

InPrivate Browsing starts in a new window and all tabs in that window are protected. If you open another browser window, that window will not be protected.

**219**

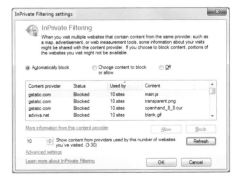

**2** Select Safety, then InPrivate Filtering settings

## Don't forget

InPrivate Filtering analyses web content on the web pages you visit, and if it sees the same content being used on a number of websites, it can block that content.

**3** To turn off InPrivate Filtering, select Off (or reselect Safety, InPrivate Filtering to remove the tick mark)

# Fix My Settings

You can make changes to your Internet settings that result in your system becoming insecure. For example:

**1** Click Tools, Internet Options and the Security tab, and click Custom Level. Select an option labelled as not secure

**2** Click OK, then Yes to change the setting

**3** Internet Explorer now displays an Information bar warning, and puts a message as home page

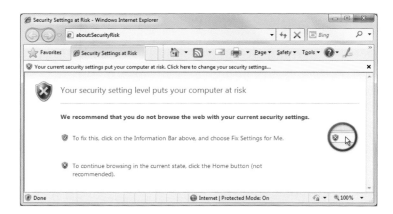

**4** Click the Information Bar and select Fix Settings for Me

**5** Click the Fix Settings button to confirm, and your settings will be restored to the defaults

# Windows Update

**1** Click Control Panel, System and Security, Windows Update (or Start, All Programs, Windows Update)

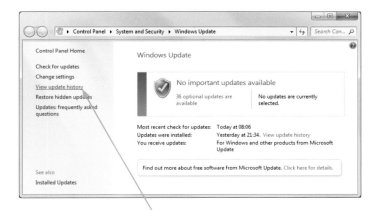

Hot tip

Windows Update provides you with online updates to keep your computer up-to-date with the latest security fixes.

**2** Click the View Update History link to see a list of all the updates that have been applied to your system

Don't forget

Click Change Settings and choose Microsoft Update, to receive updates for Office as well as for Windows.

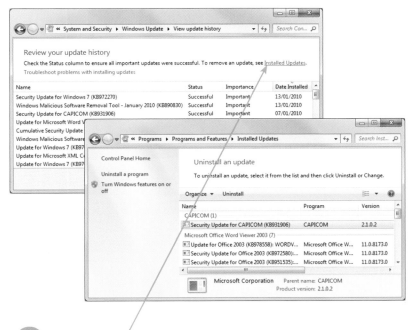

**3** Click Installed Updates to view the important updates and, if necessary, uninstall selected updates

# Firewall and Malware

**1** Select Start, Control Panel, System and Security and then Review your computer's status

## Hot tip

When Action Center opens, click the arrow next to System to display the details.

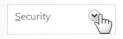

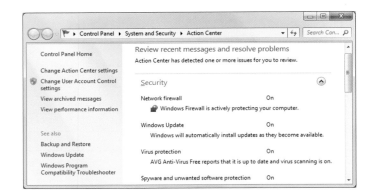

**2** Both Firewall and Malware protection should be On

**3** Automatic updating should also be On, if your system is connected via ADSL or Cable

## Don't forget

You need Firewall software to prevent other systems from accessing your computer when you are on the Internet.

Windows 7 includes built-in Firewall software, along with Windows Defender, to protect against spyware. There's no Antivirus software included in Windows. If no third-party product was supplied with your system, you can download the AVG Free Edition antivirus software from free.avg.com, for personal use, or software from other suppliers, including Symantec, Sophos and McAfee.

## Don't forget

Antivirus software detects any malicious software that may get onto your system. It can prevent or undo any harmful effects.

# Website Directory

*These are websites from across the world that are of particular interest to seniors, to help you continue your exploration of the Internet.*

# 50 Plus Information

### AARP                                     www.aarp.org

Originally the American Association of Retired Persons, AARP is a nonprofit, nonpartisan membership organization for people aged 50 and over, whether retired or not. U.S. citizenship is not required for membership.

### CARP                                     www.carp.ca

This is the Canada's association for fifty-plus, and it aims to promote the rights and quality of life for mature Canadians.

### Friendly4Seniors          www.friendly4seniors.com

An excellent resource, with over 2000 websites that are reviewed and approved as senior related, prior to listing. You can search for sites by category, state or keywords.

### Silver Surfers              www.silversurfers.net

This was created for the UK, but does have an international flavour. It is an interface to some of the best websites for the over 50s, with links to over 10,000 – British and worldwide.

**Don't forget**

There's a website associated with CARP at www.50plus.com

**Hot tip**

The websites are mainly related to US states and Canadian provinces, plus some international listings.

# Communicating

## Classmates Online     www.classmates.com

Classmates Online connects members throughout the US and Canada with friends and acquaintances from school, work and the military. Its Classmates International subsidiary operates in Sweden, France, Austria and Germany.

## People Search     www.whowhere.com

If you want to track down an acquaintance in the United States, not necessarily an old school or army mate, this search website will help you find the latest contact data. You can use it to also find the name and address for a contact when you have the phone number.

## Friends Reunited     www.friendsreunited.co.uk

You may be able to locate some of your old classmates by registering at Friends Reunited. The site lets you select and make an entry under your school, university, club or armed forces for several, mainly commonwealth, countries.

## Forces Reunited     www.forcesreunited.org.uk

For the British Armed Forces Community, it offers forums, chat, military news competitions, genealogy and access to discounts for the military. You do not have to have served in the armed forces to join.

### Hot tip

When you look back and realize how many people you have lost touch with over the years, perhaps you'll feel the urge to find out where they are now, and what has happened to them.

### Hot tip

The Lycos WhoWhere people search is just one of the many directory based websites that allow you to search for people (and businesses).

# Digital Photography

### Photographic Walks  www.all-free-photos.com

A collection of over 2,500 high resolution images of European walks and travels, in galleries of castles and parks, towns and villages, landscapes and panoramic views.

### Tips  www.digital-photography-tips.net

The site contains articles, tutorials, help with choosing a digital camera, a glossary and much more. Difficult scenarios, such as low light and night photography, are covered.

### More Tips  www.internetbrothers.com

Visit the PhotoTips page at the Internet Brothers website for another selection of digital photography tips and tutorials. For example, there is a step-by-step guide on how to take a series of overlapping digital photos and turn them into a 360° panorama video.

# Learning

### OpenLearn     www.open.ac.uk/openlearn

A learning resource from the Open
University. The site is available to anyone,
anywhere in the world. The source
material comes from the Open University, is designed for
distance learning and is free. OpenLearn is principally
for informal study. You do not need to register, but it is
recommended that you do.

### Online University     www.education-portal.com

Search for the article titled Colleges and Universities that
Offer Free Courses Online, for a list of institutions that have
decided to make course materials, including lectures, tests,
notes and readings, available for free on the Internet.

### Online School     www.free-ed.net

Free-Ed.Net is an online
school that offers nearly
two hundred career and
academic courses. Normally,
there is no sign-up and there is no cost to you. However,
Free-Ed cannot offer diplomas or certificate of completion.

### Ted     www.ted.com

A non-profit organization devoted to Ideas Worth
Spreading. Originally for Technology, Entertainment and
Design, its scope now includes global issues, business and
science. It offers fascinating talks by
well known people, and is free.

**Don't forget**

OpenLearn does
not grant awards or
credits, require you
to become an Open
University student or
offer tutorial support.

**Hot tip**

The list includes world-
class institutions like
MIT, Stanford, Yale and
UC-Berkeley.

**Don't forget**

You can get TED talks
with RSS Feeds. They
are currently translated
into 63 languages.

**Hot tip**

Exploritas promises behind-the-scenes and in-depth experiences for its cultural tours and study cruises.

## Exploritas       www.exploritas.org

Originally Elderhostel, this is a not-for-profit educational travel organization, providing opportunities for international travel, with 8,000 offerings a year in more than 90 countries.

## SeniorNet       www.seniornet.org

SeniorNet is aimed at computer-using adults, age 50 and older. It supports over 240 Learning Centres throughout the U.S. and in other countries, publishes newsletters and instructional materials, and offers online e-courses on a variety of subjects.

## U3A       www.harrowu3a.co.uk/u3a_sites.html

U3A (University of the Third Age) is an international organization whose aims are the education and stimulation of retired members of the community. The Harrow U3A maintains a list, by country, of links to U3A worldwide and other institutes for learning in retirement.

**Don't forget**

If you have skills and knowledge in any area, U3A gives you the opportunity to teach others and share your expertise.

# For Children

## How Stuff Works     www.howstuffworks.com

A subsidiary of Discovery Communications, the site offers information on anything from cosmetics to stem cell research. The website has become a recognized source of easy to understand explanations and also has quizzes and puzzles.

Hot tip

Founded originally by North Carolina State University, the site has won multiple awards.

## Online Art Lessons     www.kinderart.com

KinderArt is a large collection of free online art lessons, ideas and resources which have been contributed by people from around the world

## Museum of Natural History     www.amnh.org

The American Museum of Natural History website provides help in planning your visits, offers online resources to supplement its special exhibitions and includes a section designed for Kids & Families

Hot tip

If there's a museum near you, search on the Internet for its associated website.

## Reading and Games     www.seussville.com

If your grandchildren love The Cat in The Hat, go to the Seussville site for some games with the colorful Seussville characters.

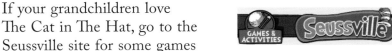

# Publishing on the Internet

### Accessibility Initiative     www.w3.org/wai /quicktips/overview.php

Seniors know better than most how web pages can become unreadable, due to poor color, contrast, etc. This overview summarizes the key concepts of accessible web design (e.g. a site suitable for the visually impaired) as a set of quick tips.

### Piers Anthony     www.hipiers.com/publishing.html

Piers Anthony (the writer of the Xanth fantasy series) and his blog-style survey of Internet publishers may be useful, when you finish that novel you've always meant to write.

### Weblog Awards     www.bloggies.com

This website tells you how to nominate weblogs for the various categories, gives details of the judging procedure and lists the finalists and the winning entry for each category.